Steck Vaughn

Teacher's Guide
Level E

FOCUS
ON SCIENCE

Harcourt Achieve
Rigby • Steck-Vaughn

www.HarcourtAchieve.com
1.800.531.5015

ISBN-13: 978-0-7398-9154-4
ISBN-10: 0-7398-9154-5

© 2004 Harcourt Achieve Inc.

All rights reserved. Harcourt Achieve Inc. grants permission to duplicate enough copies of the reproducible pages to distribute to students. Other than these specifically allowed pages, no part of the material protected by this copyright may be reproduced or utilized in any form or by any means, in whole or in part, without permission in writing from the copyright owner. Requests for permission should be mailed to: Copyright Permission, Harcourt Achieve Inc., PO Box 26015, Austin, Texas 78755.

Rigby and Steck-Vaughn are trademarks of Harcourt Achieve Inc. registered in the United States of America and/or other jurisdictions.

7 8 9 10 0930 12 11 10

Contents

About the Program

Introduction to Focus on Science

Focus on Science has been developed with both students and teachers in mind. The program presents important science concepts in language that is comfortable for on-level readers, as well as readers who read as much as one year below grade level. The content is engaging, and students are given frequent opportunities to satisfy their natural curiosity and sense of wonder through hands-on activities. The consistent lesson, exercise, and activity pages allow students to focus upon developing their science understanding.

Developed in accordance with the *National Science Education Standards* and the *Benchmarks for Scientific Literacy*, *Focus on Science* presents meaningful science content in lessons that fit easily into any instructional schedule.

About the Student Editions

The individual features in *Focus on Science* have been designed to promote student success. Students will find the style appealing and the content easy to use. Controlled vocabulary, carefully selected illustrations, and meaningful science activities work together to provide a positive learning experience for students.

Format

The student's text has three units—Life Science, Earth Science, and Physical Science. Each unit and chapter opens with an appealing photograph and brief text that encourages reflection and discussion. The opening page of each chapter also introduces the large science concepts students will encounter in their reading and activities. Six lessons follow each chapter opener. Lessons present science concepts in terms that students can understand and use illustrations and photographs to strengthen the learning process.

Hands-On Activities

Because children learn science by doing science, each chapter in *Focus on Science* provides students with a meaningful hands-on activity. These activities have been designed to maximize learning, while minimizing the demand for equipment. Important science concepts are the foundation for each activity. Activities combine carefully selected language and illustrations to guide students in independent discovery and learning. They also offer opportunities to practice problem-solving and process skills within a reasonable amount of time and with few materials.

Readability

In most classrooms, students vary widely in their reading skill development. *Focus on Science* recognizes skill diversity and presents science concepts precisely, but in an engaging style. Consequently, students will find the content manageable and interesting.

The reading level is carefully controlled at or below grade level. Important terms are defined in context, and supporting charts, diagrams, illustrations, and photographs enhance comprehension.

Text	Reading Level
Level A	Grade 1
Level B	Grade 2
Level C	Grades 2–3
Level D	Grade 3
Level E	Grade 4
Level F	Grade 5

Vocabulary

Important science terms are highlighted in boldfaced type and defined in the context of the lesson in which they first appear. The words are also arranged alphabetically in the glossary.

Illustrations

For students who rely upon visual clues for better understanding of what they read, *Focus on Science* uses illustrations, photographs, diagrams, and charts to reinforce important terms and concepts.

Special Features

Several special features have been designed to foster student interest in science. To emphasize that inquiry is the driving force in science, lesson titles are presented as questions. The questions encourage students to recall prior learning, seek more information, and ask more questions.

To reveal how science leads us from one question to another, the final section of each exercise page poses a critical-thinking question whose answer cannot be found directly in the text at hand.

At levels C through F, to show students how clues can lead to understanding, each unit begins with an intriguing task. Simple clues follow the question, "What is it?" Students may answer that question independently, or, as scientists often do, with the cooperation of their peers.

Finally, to demonstrate that science is done by many people in many settings, a Career Page appears at the conclusion of each unit. Text and photographs introduce some of the interesting science careers students may choose to pursue.

Assessment and Evaluation

Students engaged in active learning need frequent opportunities to assess their progress. Each lesson in *Focus on Science* is followed by an exercise with several sections. The first sections evaluate students' understanding of terms and concepts within the lesson. Questions appear in the order in which their answers are presented in the text. The final section of the exercise offers students practice in critical thinking. Answers to objective and critical-thinking questions are provided in the Teacher's Guide.

Focus on Science recognizes that many students benefit from experience in taking standardized tests. Consequently, comprehensive chapter and unit tests are designed to assess student learning through multiple-choice questions.

About the Teacher's Guide

The separate Teacher's Guide includes
- instructional strategies for presenting chapters and units,
- suggestions for engaging students in chapter and unit studies,
- further strategies for presenting features such as hands-on activities and career pages,
- suggestions for concluding chapter and unit studies and establishing connections to other curricular areas, and
- convenient blackline masters that extend student learning. Supporting blackline masters are identified. Simple answer keys for exercises and tests are included.

Blackline Masters

Skills Program

A successful science student acquires valuable problem-solving and process skills. *Focus on Science* offers students opportunities to develop these skills through guided questioning and participation in carefully designed, enjoyable activities. A blackline master dedicated to problem-solving and process skill development accompanies each chapter.

Chapter Reviews

Students benefit from frequent opportunities to organize their learning and review concepts. Chapter reviews present science concepts in a format unlike other activities, giving students an opportunity to review their understanding in new ways. Each chapter review is presented on a blackline master for convenience.

Unit Projects

Special unit projects, presented on blackline masters, provide creative learning extensions. They are also designed to promote independent learning. Students will be able to work successfully with little guidance from a teacher. Older children may also be encouraged to assess their performance using the easy-to-implement rubrics included in the Teacher's Guide.

Letters to Families

Because family involvement contributes positively to every student's success, a letter introducing each chapter is offered on a blackline master. These letters, written in both English and Spanish, keep family members informed and offer specific suggestions for activities that support instructional goals.

Meet your state standards with free blackline masters and links to other materials at **www.HarcourtAchieve.com/AchievementZone**. Click **Steck-Vaughn Standards**.

National Science Education Standards and Benchmarks for Scientific Literacy

National Science Education Standards recognize the cognitive development of students. The Standards in this chart are preceded by the grade levels where they have been determined as most appropriate.

Most of the Benchmarks for Scientific Literacy fit naturally in the framework of Science Education Standards. In this chart, specific Benchmarks receive special recognition as related to, but independent from the Standards. These Benchmarks are marked with an asterisk*.

National Science Education Standards and Benchmarks for Scientific Literacy	Level A	Level B	Level C	Level D	Level E	Level F
Unifying concepts and processes in science						
K–8 Systems, order, and organization	4	4	2	1,3,4	1–3	1,2,6
K–8 Evidence, models, and explanation			2	1–7	1–8	2,5,6
K–8 Change, constancy, and measurement				3,4,5	2	6
K–8 Evolution and equilibrium		4		3	2	
K–8 Form and function	2	1,2		1,3,4	2,3	
Science as Inquiry						
K–8 Abilities necessary to do scientific inquiry	1–6	4,5,6	1,3,5,6	1,2,4	1,2,6,7	1,2,4–8
K–8 Understandings about scientific inquiry	5,6	4,5,6	5,6	3,5,6,7	3,4,5,8	1–7
Physical Science						
K–4 Properties of objects and materials	6		6	7		
K–4 Position and motion of objects		6		7		8
K–4 Light, heat, electricity, and magnetism	6	6	6	7		7
5–8 Changes in properties of matter	6					7
5–8 Motions and forces					8	
5–8 Transfer of energy		6	7		7	
Life Science						
K–4 Characteristics of organisms	1,2	1,2	1–4	1,2		
K–4 Life cycles of organisms	1	1,2	1,2,4	2		
K–4 Organisms and environments	1,2,4,5	1,2,4,5	1,2,4,5	3		4
5–8 Structure and function in living systems			1	4	1,3	1,2
5–8 Reproduction and heredity					1	1,2,3
5–8 Regulation and behavior					2	
5–8 Populations and ecosystems				4	4	4
5–8 Diversity and adaptations of organisms				4	2	
*Basic function				2,3	3	2,3
*Human development				2,3		3
*Learning				2		
*Human identity				2		

National Science Education Standards and Benchmarks for Scientific Literacy (continued)

National Science Education Standards and Benchmarks for Scientific Literacy	Level A	Level B	Level C	Level D	Level E	Level F
Earth and Space Science						
K–4 Properties of Earth materials		4,5	5	5	5	
K–4 Objects in the sky	4,5	5		6		6
K–4 Changes in Earth and sky	4,5	4,5	6	5,6		5,6
5–8 Structure of Earth system					4,5	5
5–8 Earth's history						5
5–8 Earth in the solar system				6		6
Science and Technology						
K–4 Abilities to distinguish between natural and human-made objects			7	6,7	5,7,8	
K–8 Abilities of technological design				7	8	
K–8 Understandings about science and technology			6	6,7	5,7,8	
Science in Personal and Social Perspectives						
K–8 Personal health	3	3	3			
*Human Organism	3	3	2	3	3	3
*Physical health	3	3	3	3	3	3
K–4 Characteristics and changes in populations						
*Group behavior				4,5		
K–4 Science and technology in local challenges			4,5,7			4,8
5–8 Populations, resources, and environments			6,7			
*Agriculture					1,5	
5–8 Natural hazards					5	
5–8 Science and technology in society					5	8
*Global interdependence				4,5		
History and Nature of Science						
K–8 Science as a human endeavor				1–7	1–8	8
*Science as a human endeavor				1–7	1–8	8

Content Themes

	Life Science	Earth Science	Physical Science
Level A	Plants are living things Animals are living things About your body	What Earth is like Looking at the sky	Everything is made of matter
Level B	Plants react to their surroundings Animals react to their surroundings How to stay well	Earth has changed over time The sun	Energy has many forms
Level C	Plants grow and change Animals grow and change Keeping bones and muscles healthy	Plants, animals, and people depend on one another Rocks, minerals, and soil Weather and the water cycle	People get energy and materials from natural and recycled resources
Level D	Plants can make their own food There are many kinds of animals We learn about the world through our senses	Communities of living things in an ecosystem Landforms and oceans The solar system	Light, sound, magnetism, and electricity
Level E	Plants have changed over time Animals have changed over time The body has many systems	Earth has many biomes Earth's resources Weather and weather prediction	Energy can change from one form to another There are six simple machines
Level F	Plants reproduce in different ways Animal cells can perform a variety of functions Your body has control systems	Plants and animals are interdependent The changing Earth The universe and deep space	Physical and chemical properties of matter Electricity and magnetism can produce electrical energy

Lesson Scope and Sequence

Unit 1—Life Science   Chapter 1 Plants Over Time

Lesson 1	Lesson 2	Lesson 3	Lesson 4	Lesson 5	Lesson 6
The first plants were different from plants today.	The first land plants were descendants of water plants.	Vascular plants have xylem and phloem.	Flowering plants produce flowers.	As partners on Earth, plants and animals have changed.	People farm and make hybrid plants.

Chapter 2 Animals Over Time

Lesson 1	Lesson 2	Lesson 3	Lesson 4	Lesson 5	Lesson 6
The first animals were many-celled.	Fish are vertebrate animals that live in water.	Insects and amphibians moved from water to land.	Reptiles are vertebrates with dry, scaly skin.	Birds are descended from dinosaurs.	Mammals feed their young with milk.

Chapter 3 Body Systems

Lesson 1	Lesson 2	Lesson 3	Lesson 4	Lesson 5	Lesson 6
Your skeleton gives shape and support to your body.	Blood is made of plasma, blood cells, and platelets.	Your circulatory system moves blood through your body.	Your respiratory system helps you breathe.	Your digestive system turns the food you eat into fuel.	Your excretory system removes waste from your body.

Unit 2—Earth Science   Chapter 4 Biomes

Lesson 1	Lesson 2	Lesson 3	Lesson 4	Lesson 5	Lesson 6
Biomes are places with certain climates and life forms.	The tundra and the taiga are the two coldest biomes.	Deserts are the driest biomes.	Grasslands are dry biomes that get more rain than deserts.	Trees grow close together in a forest biome.	Plants and animals live in aquatic biomes.

Chapter 5 Earth's Resources

Lesson 1	Lesson 2	Lesson 3	Lesson 4	Lesson 5	Lesson 6
Resources help people meet their needs.	We use soil by growing plants in it.	We use minerals to build many things.	We use fossil fuels for the energy they provide.	Animals take in oxygen; plants take in carbon dioxide.	Living things use water in many ways.

Chapter 6 Weather

Lesson 1	Lesson 2	Lesson 3	Lesson 4	Lesson 5	Lesson 6
The atmosphere surrounds Earth.	Clouds and rain form as part of the water cycle.	Air pressure pushes against the air around you.	Wind blows between high- and low-pressure places.	A front is a zone where two different air masses meet.	Meteorologists collect information about weather.

Unit 3—Physical Science   Chapter 7 How Energy Changes

Lesson 1	Lesson 2	Lesson 3	Lesson 4	Lesson 5	Lesson 6
Temperature measures the heat energy of an object.	Heat moves through conduction, convection, and radiation.	Energy moves in different ways.	Energy can change form.	The sun is the main source of our energy.	Energy from the sun forms the electromagnetic spectrum.

Chapter 8 Simple Machines

Lesson 1	Lesson 2	Lesson 3	Lesson 4	Lesson 5	Lesson 6
Force is a push or a pull.	Force changes the motion of an object that is moving.	A lever is a bar that moves around a fixed point.	A wheel and axle is a simple machine.	A pulley is a rope looped around the wheel of a wheel and axle.	An inclined plane is a slope that makes it easier to lift an object.

Master Materials List for Hands-On Activities

Please pay particular attention when students are using sharp objects and/or handling hazardous materials in the Hands-On Activities. Advise them to use such materials cautiously.

Activity	Materials and Quantities	Special Notes
Chapter 1 **Observe Growing Plants** (p. 20)	cups—2 for class to share soil—enough to fill cups seeds—4 for each cup (total of 8) water—enough to keep both cups damp notebook—1 for each student rulers—several for class to share	A ruler is also required in Chapters 4, 6, and 8.
Chapter 2 **Make a Model of a Fossil** (p. 36)	gelatin cube—1 for each group of 4 students seashell—1 for each group of 4 students bowls—2 for each group of 4 students modeling clay—for the bottom of bowls running water—enough for each bowl	Bowls are also required in Chapter 5. Modeling clay is also required in Chapter 3.

Chapter 3
Make a Model of a Lung
(p. 52)
	safety goggles, 1-liter soda bottle, large
	    balloon, small balloon, drinking
	    straw—1 each for each student
	scissors—1 pair for each student
	tape—enough to seal each bottle
	modeling clay—enough to seal each straw
		Safety goggles are also required in Chapter 5. Scissors are also required in Chapter 6. Tape is also required in Chapters 4, 6, and 8.

Chapter 4 **Make a Rainfall Gauge** (p. 70)	coffee or large juice can, inch ruler, paper, pencil—1 each for each student tape—enough to tape rulers to cans	Paper and pencil are also required in Chapters 6 and 8.

Chapter 5
Recycle Paper
(p. 86)
	newspapers, water, plastic wrap, large
	    books—as needed for each group
	safety goggles—1 for each student
	laundry starch—2 teaspoons for each group
	screen, teaspoon, flat pan, small bowl, large
	    bowl, stirring stick—1 for each group
		This can be a messy activity. Explain that all resources are valuable. Students should try not to spill materials.

Chapter 6 **Make a Wind Speed Indicator** (p. 102)	protractor, paper, pencil, centimeter ruler, foam ball, scissors—1 for each student string—1 20-cm piece for each student stapler—1 for the class to share tape—as needed	

Chapter 7
Observe Convection
(p. 120)
	tall plastic cups, short plastic cups—2 of
	    each for each group of 4 students
	cold and hot water—as needed
	food coloring—as needed
	spoon, dropper—1 for each group
	    of 4 students	

Chapter 8
Test Friction
(p. 136)
	paper, pencil, ruler, book, wood block,
	    construction paper, sandpaper—1 for
	    each student
	tape—enough to tape surfaces to books
	aluminum foil—1 piece for each student
		Conduct the same activity with a toy car (that is similar in weight to the wood block) to illustrate how wheels reduce friction.

Unit Summary The first plants and animals were very different from life on Earth today. They lived in the ocean and were very simple creatures. Gradually, they moved onto land and developed many new forms. These included vascular plants, and animals such as birds, reptiles, insects, amphibians, and mammals. The human body has many systems that make it work.

Before Reading the Unit Ask students to suggest where they think the first life on Earth developed. As you discuss this, encourage students to tell what they think the earliest forms of plant and animal life may have looked like. Point out that it took millions and millions of years for life to move from water onto the land and millions more for the huge variety of life we know today to develop.

Unit Performance Project

Setup and Presentation Page 52 in the Teacher's Guide contains a reproducible project that focuses on changes in plants and animals over time. Present this project after students have completed Chapter 2. Before students begin the project, you may wish to review with them the kinds of plants and animals that are covered in the chapter.

Evaluation A satisfactory project should show examples of different groups of plants and animals.

A good project should show all the main groups of plants and animals placed accurately on the timeline.

An outstanding project should show detailed drawings that have been placed correctly on the timeline. Each drawing should be labeled and fully explained. There is a rubric on page 55 in this Teacher's Guide that will assist students in evaluating their own work on the unit performance project.

Careers Feature

Page 54 of the student text offers students a glimpse into the careers of a botanist, herpetologist, and respiratory therapist. Explain to students that to be a botanist or herpetologist, they will want to learn a great deal about plant and animal life. Both of these careers require a four-year college degree, and many people in these fields also pursue an advanced degree. A botanist might work in agriculture, forestry, horticulture, or pharmacology. A herpetologist might work at a zoo or in conservation. Both of these professionals might also do research or teach. To be a respiratory therapist, students will need a thorough understanding of the human body and be able to work well with people. This career usually requires a two-year course at a community college and on-the-job training. Have students choose the field that interests them most. Encourage them to find out more about the work involved and the preparation they would need to enter the field. When students have finished their research, invite them to discuss in small groups what they have learned.

Unit Test The Blackline Master for Unit 1 Test is on page 46 of the Teacher's Guide. The test is in the standardized test format to provide students with practice in taking standardized tests. The unit test content focuses on the development of plant and animal life from their earliest forms, as well as the systems in the human body.

Answers: 1. C 2. A 3. B 4. B 5. C 6. B 7. A 8. C 9. A 10. D

After Reading the Unit Help students relate the information in this unit to their everyday lives. Ask: How does knowing about the ways that different groups of plants and animals developed help you understand more about the world around you? How does learning more about body systems help you understand your body and health better? Has any of the information in this unit affected your behavior or outlook on the world?

Chapter Summary The first plants lived in the oceans. Eventually, plant life moved onto land. The first land plants simply lay in damp areas near water. After millions of years, vascular plants appeared. These plants can carry water and food to all their parts. Flowering plants appeared several hundred million years later. They make seeds through pollination. Plants and animals have changed together over millions of years. People have changed plants by farming and developing hybrid plants.

Chapter Objectives Students will learn to
- describe the first plants.
- relate the properties of vascular plants.
- identify the parts of flowering plants.
- interpret how plants and animals have changed together.
- explain how people change plants.

Vocabulary

fossils, p. 8	flowering plants, p. 14
photosynthesis, p. 8	species, p. 14
extinct, p. 8	reproduce, p. 14
vascular plants, p. 12	nectar, p. 14
xylem, p. 12	pollen, p. 14
phloem, p. 12	pollination, p. 14
ferns, p. 12	domesticated plants, p. 18
conifers, p. 12	hybrid plants, p. 18

Vocabulary Activity Write the term *vascular plants* on the chalkboard. Have students use this word to begin a word web using as many of the vocabulary terms as they can. When students are finished, have them discuss the meanings of the vocabulary words they used.

Before Reading the Chapter Ask students to answer the "What Is It?" riddle in the Chapter Opener. Then, show students a fossil or photo of a fossil of an ancient plant. Ask them to describe

how they think the fossil was formed. Point out that these traces of life can date back more than a billion years. Encourage students to suggest how fossils can be useful to scientists.

Lesson 1 What Were the First Plants?
Show students photos, prepared slides, or examples of green algae. Explain that forms of this algae were probably the ancestors of the earliest plants on Earth. Discuss how sunlight does not penetrate very deeply into water so most marine plants and animals live relatively close to the surface of the world's oceans.

Answers page 9: A. 1. paleobotanists 2. billion 3. water 4. photosynthesis 5. extinct B. 3. √ 4. √ 5. √ C. The answer could include that the earliest plants decayed before fossils could form, or that rocks that may have preserved fossils have been destroyed.

Lesson 2 What Were the First Land Plants?
Focus attention on ways that water plants may have been able to move onto land. Be sure students understand that these early land plants did not look like most of the plants we know today, but were still a very important step in plant development.

Answers page 11: A. 1. water plants 2. water plants 3. land plants 4. both B. 1. ancestors 2. shores 3. pioneers C. 1. √ 2. √ 3. √ 5. √ D. No, the first land plants would not have been able to live on top of a rock sticking out of the water. They had no stems or roots, so they needed to be completely touching damp soil.

Lesson 3 What Are Vascular Plants?
Have students imagine a garden or a forest. Then ask them to suggest how the plants or trees they are visualizing are able to stand upright and get food and water to all their parts. (They have a system that can carry food and water throughout their roots, stems, and leaves.)

Answers page 13: A. 1. vascular—plants that have special tissues to carry water and food 2. xylem—tissues that carry water and nutrients through the plant 3. phloem—tissues that carry food made during photosynthesis through the plant 4. ferns—leafy plants that grow in shady, damp areas 5. conifers—plants that hold their seeds in cones B. 1. The first vascular plants looked like green stems stretching across the ground. 2. Vascular plants developed roots to hold them in the soil and to take in water. Some also developed leaves with special shapes to capture more sunlight. C. 2. √ 4. √ 5. √ D. Vascular tissues are very helpful in getting plants the water, nutrients, and food they need and in helping them grow.

Lesson 4 What Are Flowering Plants?

Encourage students to look carefully at the reproductive parts of different flowers. Then have students look at the photograph of the bee. Ask them to explain how bees spread pollen from flower to flower. (It sticks to their bodies.) Discuss how a decline in the bee population could affect flowering plants. (Plants might have more trouble reproducing.)

Answers page 15: A. 1. million 2. kinds 3. flowering plants 4. new plants 5. pollen B. 2. √ 3. √ C. They work together to get things they both need. The plant provides food for insects, and the insects help transfer pollen.

Lesson 5 How Have Plants and Animals Changed Together?

Ask students to think of examples of how plants and animals affect each other. (Many animals eat plants or eat animals that eat plants; animals carry plant seeds on their bodies; when animals die, they may help fertilize the soil that plants grow in.) Ask students to suggest how over millions of years a type of animal might become immune to a poisonous plant. (Animals might have eaten small amounts and survived. Over generations, the animals that could eat the plant and still survive could pass this trait on until more and more of the animals had it.)

Answers page 17: A. 1. True 2. True 3. True 4. True 5. False 6. False B. 1. animals 2. plants 3. food 4. sometimes 5. each other C. The animal's mouth might change so the thorns wouldn't hurt.

Lesson 6 How Do People Change Plants?

Point out that before farming, people ate only wild plants. Ask what people would have to understand about plants in order to begin farming. (Plants produce seeds, which make new plants.)

Why would farming be preferable to eating wild plants? (People need to have a steady, reliable food source. Also, when people farm, all the crop is grown in a small area, whereas wild plants must be gathered wherever they can be found.)

Answers page 19: A. 1. farmers 2. healthiest 3. purposely 4. domesticated 5. hybrid B. 1. True 2. True 3. False C. People might change some plants to make them stronger. They might change some flowering plants to make them look better, with more or larger blossoms or new shades of color.

Hands-On Activity *page 20*

Students will engage in the process skill of observing as they watch how seeds grow. Provide students with needed materials. Radish seeds work very well for this activity. Extend the activity by asking these questions: Were the plants able to grow without light? If so, where do you think they got food to grow? (Yes, the plants in the dark were able to grow. They got their food from inside the seed.) How could you change this experiment to show the effect of water on plants? (You could plant seeds in two cups and place both on the windowsill. You could water the seeds in one cup but not water the seeds in the other.)

Answers: 1. Both plants should have sprouted. However, the plant in the light should have grown faster and possibly larger. 2. Plants grow better in the light than in the dark.

Blackline Masters for Chapter 1:

Problem Solving Skill, page 30; Chapter Review, page 38; Letter to Family (English/Spanish), page 56

"What Is It?" *Answer:* vascular plant

Chapter Test *page 21*

Answers: 1. A 2. D 3. B 4. B 5. D 6. C 7. A 8. B 9. C 10. A

After Reading the Chapter

Geography Have students make a map of where flowers grow around their homes. Tell students to make several 15-minute observations at one place on their maps and record how many insects appear. Then ask them to estimate how many insects visit all the places where flowers grow in one 8-hour day.

Chapter Summary The first animals appeared about 600 million years ago. They were soft-bodied, many-celled creatures. Over millions of years these animals developed first into invertebrate, hard-bodied ocean animals, and then into fish. Fish were the first animals with skeletons. The first animals to live on land were insects. Amphibians followed, and eventually developed into reptiles and birds. Mammals are the most recent development. They are vertebrates that have hair on their bodies and feed their young with milk.

Chapter Objectives Students will learn to
- describe the first animals.
- understand the early development of fish.
- relate the characteristics of insects, amphibians, and reptiles.
- recount the properties of dinosaurs and birds.
- identify characteristics of mammals.

Vocabulary

soft-bodied, p. 24	cartilage, p. 26
hard-bodied, p. 24	bony fish, p. 26
invertebrates, p. 26	insects, p. 28
vertebrates, p. 26	amphibians, p. 28
jawless fish, p. 26	reptiles, p. 30
jawed fish, p. 26	dinosaurs, p. 32

Vocabulary Activity Have students draw two columns on a piece of paper. One column should be headed *vertebrates* and the other *invertebrates*. Then, have students classify the other vocabulary words under the appropriate category. When students have finished their lists, have them work with a partner or in small groups to compare their lists and discuss why each word belongs to its category.

Before Reading the Chapter Ask students to volunteer answers to the "What Is It?" riddle in the Chapter Opener. Then, encourage students to think of the great variety of animal life on Earth. You might ask them to name different types of animals. Write their responses on the chalkboard. Point out that there are billions of animals all over the planet, including fish, insects, reptiles, birds, and mammals, but that it took many hundreds of millions of years for these species to develop from their earliest forms of life.

Lesson 1 What Were the First Animals?
Explain to students that just as plants grew from very simple organisms, so did animals. Encourage students to suggest what the first kinds of animals might have been like and where they probably lived. (simple many-celled animals with soft bodies—some similar to jellyfish; in the oceans)
    Answers page 25: A. 1. False 2. False 3. False B. 1. bacteria 2. many-celled 3. soft-bodied C. 1. one-celled—made up of just one cell 2. many-celled—made up of more than one cell 3. soft-bodied—animals without bones or shells 4. hard-bodied—animals with bones or shells 5. trilobites—early animals that crawled on the bottom of the ocean D. Hard body coverings can protect animals from their enemies.

Lesson 2 What Are Fish?
Show students live fish or photos of different kinds of fish. Use the fish and photos as prompts to discuss how fish are similar to and different from one another. Ask students to suggest how the bodies of fish are supported. Elicit the idea that most—but not all—fish have bony skeletons that support their bodies.
    Answers page 27: A. 3, 4, 2, 1 B. 1. invertebrates 2. vertebrates 3. ostracoderms 4. jawless fish 5. jawed fish 6. cartilage 7. bony fish C. Jawed fish could eat more kinds of food.

Lesson 3 What Are Insects and Amphibians?
Ask students to tell which group of animals they think is the most plentiful on Earth. Use the responses to help students understand the incredible numbers of insects that live on Earth. Then ask them to discuss the similarities among frogs, toads, and salamanders. (They live part of their lives in the water and part on land.)

Point out that these animals were the first vertebrates to live on land.

Answers page 29: A. 1. True 2. False 3. True 4. True 5. True 6. False B. 1. million 2. six 3. insects 4. millions 5. part C. Perhaps food in their water environment was becoming scarce, or the water was becoming polluted or drying up. They most likely moved to find a new source of water or food.

Lesson 4 What Are Reptiles?

Ask students to choose a reptile and make a drawing of it. Encourage students to find illustrations to use as examples. When they have finished, ask them to share their work and talk about how reptiles are different from other animals.

Answers page 31: A. 1. backbones 2. amphibians 3. on land 4. salamanders 5. pterosaurs 6. million B. 1. both 2. amphibians 3. reptiles 4. reptiles C. Amphibians and reptiles both need water to live. Amphibians also need to lay their eggs in water.

Lesson 5 What Are Dinosaurs and Birds?

Ask students to consider how birds developed. As students reply, encourage them to support their ideas with evidence. (Two points are that both birds and reptiles have eggs with shells, and that many birds have three reptile-like claws on each leg. Differences are that birds have feathers and are warm-blooded, while reptiles are cold-blooded.) Discuss how archaeopteryx was a step in the development from reptiles to modern birds.

Answers page 33: A. 1. True 2. True 3. False 4. False 5. False B. 1. reptiles 2. reptiles 3. feathers 4. archaeopteryx 5. bird 6. crow C. Many people have found dinosaurs very interesting because several dinosaurs were big and fierce and because they no longer exist.

Lesson 6 What Are Mammals?

Discuss the concept of extinction. You might begin with examples of ancient animals that no longer exist, such as dinosaurs. Point out that adaptation often takes a very long time, sometimes millions of years, and that Earth today is changing very rapidly. Ask students to describe the kinds of adaptations that might have to occur due to changing climates, air and water pollution, and reduced open space. Ask them how these changes might affect the ability of

animals to adapt. (The rapid speed of change makes adaptation very difficult.)

Answers page 35: A. 2. √ 3. √ 4. √ B. 1. different conditions 2. Mammals 3. survive 4. an adaptation 5. become extinct C. A deer's adaptations include body coloring that hides it from its enemies and long, thin legs that give it the ability to run fast.

Hands-On Activity *page 36* Students will engage in the process skill of modeling as they make a model of a fossil. Provide students with the needed materials. Make gelatin cubes by preparing gelatin and cutting it into 1-inch cubes. If running water is not available in your classroom, you can pour water from a gallon jug into the bowls and drain them into a clean wastebasket.

Answers: 1. The gelatin cube represented an animal with soft body parts, while the seashell represented an animal with hard body parts. 2. Only the seashell left a fossil because some of the gelatin washed away, and what was left was too soft to make an impression in the clay. 3. Answers may vary. Students may suggest placing a seashell, chicken bone, or other hard object inside the gelatin cube.

Blackline Masters for Chapter 2:

Problem Solving Skill, page 31; Chapter Review, page 39; Letter to Family (English/Spanish), page 57

"What Is It?" *Answer:* reptile

Chapter Test *page 37*

Answers: 1. A 2. A 3. A 4. C 5. C 6. D 7. B 8. C 9. A 10. B

After Reading the Chapter

Math On page 28 the text stated that if all the insects in the world were spread evenly across Earth, there would be more than 2 billion insects in every square mile. Ask students to calculate about how many insects would be in each square foot. (Sq. mi. = 5,280 ft. x 5,280 ft. = 27,878,400 sq. ft.; 2 billion divided by 27,878,400 = about 72 insects)

Chapter Summary The skeletal system gives shape and support to the body. The circulatory system moves blood throughout the body. Blood carries oxygen and carbon dioxide and helps fight disease. The respiratory system provides oxygen to the body and removes carbon dioxide. The digestive system turns food into fuel. The excretory system passes waste water and chemicals out of the body.

Chapter Objectives Students will learn to

- explain the skeletal system.
- relate some properties of blood.
- describe the circulatory system.
- identify the respiratory system.
- explain the digestive system.
- understand the excretory system.

Vocabulary

bones, p. 40	veins, p. 44
muscles, p. 40	capillaries, p. 44
joints, p. 40	respiratory system, p. 46
involuntary muscles, p. 40	trachea, p. 46
voluntary muscles, p. 40	lungs, p. 46
tendons, p. 40	diaphragm, p. 46
blood, p. 42	digestive system, p. 48
plasma, p. 42	stomach, p. 48
red blood cells, p. 42	intestines, p. 48
white blood cells, p. 42	saliva, p. 48
platelets, p. 42	esophagus, p. 48
carbon dioxide, p. 42	excretory system, p. 50
blood vessels, p. 44	bladder, p. 50
arteries, p. 44	kidneys, p. 50
circulatory system, p. 44	

Vocabulary Activity Divide the class into small groups. Provide each group with a body outline cut from art paper (butcher paper). Then, when the students complete each lesson, have them draw and label the lesson's body system on the pattern. They should use all of their vocabulary words.

Before Reading the Chapter Ask students to volunteer answers to the "What Is It?" riddle in the Chapter Opener. Then, ask them to think of parts of the body that work whether they are asleep or awake, or that work without conscious effort. (lungs, heart, stomach, eyes, ears) Then ask students to think of parts of the body that we can consciously control. (some muscles, parts of the brain) Discuss why some parts of the body need to work without our control.

Lesson 1 What Is Your Skeletal System?
Have students move their arms, fingers, necks, and hands. Explain that they are using different muscles to move their bones and that the points at which the bones are connected are called joints. Explain that even a simple movement like moving the hands and fingers can use about 20 muscles and that when we walk we use more than 100 muscles.

Answers page 41: A. 1. muscles 2. protect 3. joints 4. tendons 5. relaxes B. 1. V 2. I 3. I 4. V C. No, the joint would not work correctly. Without the tendon to attach the muscles to the bone, the muscles would not be able to pull the bone to move the joint.

Lesson 2 What Is Blood?
Ask students to suggest reasons why blood circulates through our bodies. (to provide oxygen, carry off carbon dioxide, and provide food) Direct attention to the illustration on page 42 of the student textbook. Discuss the differences between red and white blood cells and the important jobs that each of these types of cells do.

Answers page 43: A. 1. Red blood cells carry oxygen to body cells. 2. White blood cells kill germs to fight disease. 3. Platelets clot blood to close wounds. B. 1. plasma 2. body 3. water 4. carbon dioxide 5. white blood cells 6. platelets 7. bones C. Platelets would create sticky threads to close the wound and stop the bleeding. This would keep any more germs from getting into the body. The white blood cells would kill any germs that had come into the wound. They would also carry away the dead germs and any dead body cells.

Lesson 3 What Is Your Circulatory System?

Have students talk about how blood is able to travel throughout the body. (The heart pumps it.) Have students study the diagram of the heart, noting how blood flows to and from the body and lungs. Elicit the idea that the circulatory system must work together with the lungs and respiratory system, which students will learn about in the next lesson.

Answers page 45: A. 1. blood vessels 2. muscle 3. carbon dioxide 4. oxygen 5. capillaries B. 3, 5, 2, 4, 1 C. The heart is an involuntary muscle that beats all the time, even when a person is asleep.

Lesson 4 What Is Your Respiratory System?

As students look at the lesson illustrations, point out that while the human body can survive without food for days, it won't last more than minutes without air.

Answers page 47: A. nose, trachea, lungs, air sacs, capillaries, diaphragm B. labels in order from the top: trachea, lungs, diaphragm C. If the piece of food is small, you might be able to breathe, but it would be difficult. If the piece of food completely blocked the trachea, you would not be able to breathe at all. You would be choking.

Lesson 5 What Is Your Digestive System?

Ask students to describe their experiences after eating lunch. (Some students may have noticed that they become slightly chilly after eating lunch; most will say that it is hard to move on a full stomach.) Stress the idea that digesting food not only gives us energy but requires a lot of energy.

Answers page 49: A. 1. mouth 2. esophagus 3. stomach 4. small intestine 5. large intestine B. 1. food 2. stomach 3. saliva 4. involuntary muscle 5. stores 6. small intestine C. The system would not work properly. It needs the involuntary muscles to push food through the esophagus and intestines. Involuntary muscles also work in the stomach to mix food.

Lesson 6 What Is Your Excretory System?

Ask students to describe what happens to their skin when they are exercising very hard.

(It sweats.) Have students suggest reasons why this takes place, helping them understand that sweat is a way for the body to both cool itself and get rid of wastewater and chemicals.

Answers page 51: A. 1. False 2. True 3. True B. 1. skin 2. bladder 3. dead cells C. 1. Waste is made by the body as it works. 2. Blood is cleaned in tiny capsules inside the kidneys. 3. Waste liquid is stored in the bladder. 4. Skin sheds waste through tiny holes. D. Since the kidneys clean blood by taking waste chemicals and water out of it, it is important to resupply the water in the body.

Hands-On Activity *page 52* Students will engage in the process skill of modeling as they use balloons to demonstrate the functions of a diaphragm and a lung. Provide students with the needed materials. Balloons that come in packages of assorted sizes and shapes are suitable for this activity.

Answers: 1. The large balloon represents the diaphragm. The small balloon represents the lungs. 2. Students should mention that when they pulled out the balloon, they modeled the diaphragm moving down, and the lungs filling with air. When they pushed in the balloon, they modeled the diaphragm moving up, and air leaving the lungs.

Blackline Masters for Chapter 3:

Problem Solving Skill, page 32; Chapter Review, page 40; Letter to Family (English/Spanish), page 58

"What Is It?" *Answer:* bone

Chapter Test *page 53*

Answers: 1. A 2. B 3. C 4. B 5. C 6. A 7. C 8. D 9. B 10. D

After Reading the Chapter

Writing Have students imagine that one of their arm or leg muscles can communicate. Then ask them to write a journal entry for this muscle. Tell students to describe several different activities the muscle is required to do from the muscle's point of view. Encourage students to use vivid descriptions to give the reader a good idea of what the muscle does.

Unit Summary Animals and plants have adapted to different biomes, or climatic regions of Earth. People use renewable and nonrenewable natural resources, such as minerals, soil, air, fossil fuels, and water, for food, clothing, shelter, and enjoyment. Changes in weather occur in the troposphere where moisture and air pressure are affected by temperature.

Before Reading the Unit Invite students to skim Unit 2, looking at the pictures and reading the headings. Tell students they will be studying life on Earth, Earth's resources, and weather patterns. Ask why people want to study Earth and its wildlife. Why do people need to know where resources come from and how to protect them? Why is knowing about the weather important?

Unit Performance Project

Setup and Presentation Page 53 in this Teacher's Guide is a reproducible project that focuses on the formation of weather patterns. Present the project as you begin studying weather (Chapter 6).

Tell students that the information they need to complete this project can be found in Unit 2. Tell them to begin with a pencil sketch, and to add arrows and captions to clearly explain each step of the process.

Evaluation A satisfactory project should include basic explanations, in drawings and captions, of the water cycle and of how a front forms when air masses of different temperatures and pressures meet. Writing should indicate an understanding that water is a renewable resource.

A good project should show details of how water evaporates to become water vapor, condenses into clouds, and then falls as rain. It should also show how a storm front forms when a cold, low pressure air mass moves under a warm, high pressure air mass. Writing should indicate an understanding that water is a renewable resource and that plants and animals—also renewable resources—require water to live.

An outstanding project should include details of each process. Drawings and writing should be careful and complete. There is a rubric on page 55 in this Teacher's Guide that will assist students in evaluating their work.

Careers Feature

Page 104 of the student text offers students a glimpse into the careers of a marine biologist, geologist, and soil conservationist. Explain that each of these fields generally requires four years of college, culminating in a degree in science. Many experts in these fields also spend at least two additional years in specialized study. To earn an advanced degree, a scientist must write a thesis on a specific area of study. For example, a marine biologist might spend two years studying the effects of sea otters on kelp beds, or a soil conservationist might experiment with methods of halting erosion. Some advanced degree programs require several years of field work or an internship with a scientific team. Suggest that students choose one of the fields to research. Have them read articles on the Internet or in recent periodicals to learn about developments in the field. Ask them to write brief reports on what they have learned.

Unit Test The Blackline Master for Unit 2 Test is on page 47 of the Teacher's Guide. The test is in the standardized test format to provide students with practice in taking standardized tests. The unit test content focuses on the climate and location of biomes, natural resources and how to protect them, and the formation of weather patterns.

Answers: 1. D 2. A 3. D 4. B 5. C 6. B 7. A 8. C 9. A 10. D

After Reading the Unit Help students relate the information in this unit to their daily lives. Ask: How does knowing about life processes help you understand plants and animals? How does knowing about Earth's resources help you make responsible decisions? How does understanding weather patterns help you understand your everyday experiences? How can you care for planet Earth?

Chapter Summary Plants and animals have adapted to different biomes. Varying amounts of annual rainfall provide habitats for specific plants. Particular animals depend on these plants for food and shelter. Earth's biomes include the cold tundra and taiga, the dry desert, and wide areas of grassland. Other kinds of biomes are forests, including deciduous and tropical rain forests, and underwater, or aquatic biomes, both saltwater and freshwater.

Chapter Objectives Students will learn to
- describe a biome.
- distinguish between the tundra and taiga.
- understand how plants and animals have adapted to the dry desert.
- identify plant and animal life in grassland biomes.
- distinguish between deciduous forests and tropical rain forests.
- explain differences in aquatic biomes.

Vocabulary

climate, p. 58	forests, p. 66
biome, p. 58	deciduous, p. 66
savanna, p. 58	rain forests, p. 66
tundra, p. 60	tropics, p. 66
taiga, p. 60	canopy, p. 66
precipitation, p. 60	aquatic biomes, p. 68
evergreens, p. 60	marine biomes, p. 68
deserts, p. 62	saltwater, p. 68
grasslands, p. 64	plankton, p. 68
burrows, p. 64	gills, p. 68

Vocabulary Activity Ask students to draw a map of North America like the one on page 58 on a large piece of paper. As students read the chapter, ask them to outline each biome on the map. Then they should add drawings that show the kinds of plants and animals that live in each biome. Tell students to add labels or captions that use all of their vocabulary words.

Before Reading the Chapter Ask students to answer the "What Is It?" riddle in the Chapter Opener. Then, ask students to talk about unusual ecosystems they have visited or unusual animals they have seen. Encourage students to share their ideas about why certain regions provide homes for particular plants and animals.

Lesson 1 What Is a Biome?
Invite a naturalist to speak to the class about the biome in which you live. Help students understand how annual rainfall affects your biome, and how plants and animals have adapted to the climate. Also discuss how your biome differs from others and where similar biomes can be found around the world.
Answers page 59: A. 1. climate 2. biome 3. climate is 4. savanna B. 1. False 2. False 3. True 4. True 5. False 6. True C. There would be less diversity among plants and animals.

Lesson 2 What Are the Tundra and the Taiga?
Use a world map to show where different biomes are located. Help students focus on the tundra and the taiga.
Answers page 61: A. 1. tundra 2. reindeer 3. arctic hare 4. taiga 5. evergreens 6. spruce B. 1. tundra 2. tundra 3. tundra 4. taiga 5. taiga C. The color change of the arctic hare's coat helps it hide from its enemies. The hare's white coat makes it harder to see against the snow during winter. The hare's coat changes to brown or gray to better hide it from its enemies when there is no snow on the ground.

Lesson 3 What Are Deserts?
To prepare for this lesson, bring in library books with photographs of desert plants and animals. Ask students to examine the photographs and identify special adaptations. Place the books in a reading corner of the classroom and invite students to read more about desert biomes.
Answers page 63: A. 1. False 2. False 3. True 4. True 5. False B. 1. deserts 2. adaptations 3. cactus 4. underground 5. night 6. ears C. By making many seeds, the plants ensure that there will be seeds left to grow when the next rain falls.

Lesson 4 What Are Grasslands?

Ask students to use an almanac to locate and list the annual rainfall figures for grassland regions in North America and in Africa. Ask students to list annual rainfall amounts for tropical rain forests and desert regions. Organize the information on a chart and compare the figures.

Answers page 65: A. 1. grasslands 2. grazing animals 3. herd 4. burrows 5. dry season 6. one third 7. wheat B. 1. gazelle—very fast runner 2. gopher—escapes to underground burrow 3. puff adder snake—color matches dry grasses C. Traveling in large numbers, as in herds, gives grazing animals some protection from their enemies.

Lesson 5 What Are Forests?

Take your students on a walk among trees. Discuss the differences and similarities between the trees the students see and trees found in tropical, evergreen, or deciduous forests. Point out other plants and animals. Then, ask students to pair up and make their own observations. Have them take detailed notes on the plants and animals they see.

Answers page 67: A. 1. rainfall 2. deciduous 3. rain forests 4. canopy 5. the canopy B. 1. D 2. R 3. R 4. R C. The climate of the rain forest makes it a good place for many plants to grow. The fruits and leaves of the abundant plant life provide food for many animals.

Lesson 6 What Are Aquatic Biomes?

As you study Lesson 6, you may want to visit an aquarium or aquarium store. Or you might show students a video on ocean or pond life. Or, if a microscope is available, invite students to look at tiny organisms living in water from a pond, river, or the ocean. You might also buy brine shrimp eggs at an aquarium store and invite students to watch the tiny shrimp hatch.

Answers page 69: A. 1. aquatic biomes 2. marine biomes 3. plankton 4. oxygen 5. freshwater biomes 6. gills B. 1. Marine 2. Marine 3. Freshwater 4. Freshwater C. The difference between a freshwater biome and a marine biome is the salt in the water, so the salt must be harmful to the brook trout.

Hands-On Activity *page 70* Students will engage in the process skills of observing and measuring precipitation as they construct a rainfall gauge. Provide students with needed materials. If your area gets little or no precipitation at this time of year, you can postpone this activity until later in the year. If your area receives snowfall instead of rainfall at this time of year, you can adjust the activity accordingly. Students should check their gauges every day at the same time for a week.

Answers: 1. Answers may vary. 2. Answers may vary. 3. Answers may vary. Accept all reasonable answers.

Blackline Masters for Chapter 4:
Problem Solving Skill, page 33; Chapter Review, page 41; Letter to Family (English/Spanish), page 59

"What Is It?" *Answer:* precipitation

Chapter Test *page 71*
Answers: 1. C 2. D 3. B 4. D 5. A 6. C 7. B 8. A 9. C 10. B

After Reading the Chapter
Social Studies Share some examples of plants like the rosy periwinkle and animals like sharks that have contributed valuable medicines. Ask students to seek more examples of plants and animals in Earth's rain forests and oceans that help people. Ask students to use the information they collect to write a speech to be presented at a meeting of the United Nations. The speech should convince listeners of the need to protect forest and ocean resources.

Writing Ask students to imagine being a scientist on board a research ship in the Pacific Ocean. They have been hired by the owner of a Peruvian fishery to find out why there has been a decline in fish catches. The owner blames El Niño. Ask the students to use the Internet and other resources to learn about El Niño. Then, have them submit a report of their findings to the fishery owner.

Chapter Summary People use Earth's natural resources for food, clothing, shelter, and enjoyment. We use plants and animals, soil, and minerals. We use fossil fuels for heat and energy. We breathe the air and drink the water. Fossil fuels and minerals are nonrenewable resources. Plants and animals, air, soil, and water are renewable resources. We need to protect all resources from overuse and pollution.

Chapter Objectives Students will learn to
- distinguish between renewable and nonrenewable resources.
- describe the composition and value of soil, how it can be polluted, and how it can be preserved.
- identify how people use minerals.
- understand fossil fuel origins and uses.
- describe the composition of air, how people pollute it, and how they protect it from pollution.
- understand why water is a precious natural resource.

Vocabulary

natural resources, p. 74	ore, p. 78
renewable resources, p. 74	fossil fuels, p. 80
nonrenewable resources, p. 74	petroleum, p. 80
	natural gas, p. 80
soil, p. 76	coal, p. 80
fertilizer, p. 76	decompose, p.80
polluted, p. 76	oxygen, p. 82
mining, p. 76	nitrogen, p. 82
erosion, p. 76	atmosphere, p. 82
compost, p. 76	gravity, p. 82
windbreaks, p. 76	carbon dioxide, p. 82
minerals, p. 78	saltwater, p. 84

Vocabulary Activity Create a bulletin board entitled *What Are Resources?* Divide the class into groups. Assign each group to write the vocabulary words on index cards and then find or draw images that correspond to each vocabulary word. Then ask the students to complete the bulletin board.

Before Reading the Chapter Ask students to volunteer answers to the "What Is It?" riddle in the Chapter Opener. Then suggest that students look around the classroom and try to explain where various items, such as books, furniture, tools, and clothing, came from. What materials were used to make them? How and where were the raw materials obtained? Point out that everything we own or use comes from resources found on Earth.

Lesson 1 What Are Resources?
Point out that *renewable* is a relative term. Explain that although soil, water, and air are called renewable, they are not inexhaustible. If we do not protect Earth's trees and plants, they will not continue to produce oxygen. If we pollute oceans and groundwater, we will reduce drinking water supplies. If large areas of soil are lost because of erosion, they cannot be replaced.
    Answers page 75: A. 1. food 2. renewable 3. nonrenewable 4. replaced 5. grow B. 1. R 2. N 3. R 4. N 5. R C. Renewable resources must be used carefully to make sure they will always be available. Nonrenewable resources must be used carefully to make them last as long as possible.

Lesson 2 How Do We Use Soil?
Take a walk with students on or near school grounds and encourage students to discover a place that is suffering from soil erosion. Talk about what may have caused the erosion. Help students plant grass seed, groundcover, or a tree. Water the plants regularly and observe the results.
    Answers page 77: A. 1. True 2. False 3. False 4. True 5. True B. 1. natural waste 2. fertilizer 3. lumber 4. mining 5. erosion C. Chemicals from rotting garbage and other materials people throw away can sink into the soil, not only at the garbage dump, but also on nearby land. These chemicals pollute the soil.

Lesson 3 How Do We Use Minerals?
Invite a rock collector, geologist, or jeweler to share mineral samples with the class. Bring in library books about minerals. Invite students to look through the books and make lists of uses

for minerals. Discuss how silicon is used in microcomputers. Point out that without this natural resource, recent developments in computer science could not have happened.

Answers page 79: A. 1. minerals 2. ore 3. remove 4. nonrenewable 5. recycle 6. glass B. 1. diamonds—used to make jewelry 2. iron—used to make steel 3. sand—used to make glass 4. aluminum—used to make cooking foil C. Gold is rarer than silver.

Lesson 4 How Do We Use Fossil Fuels?

Tell students there is a limited amount of fossil fuel, and that our present rate of consumption cannot last. Ask students to share what they know about alternative energy sources. Ask if students know companies or families in your community who get energy from solar, wind, or water power.

Answers page 81: A. 1. fossil fuels 2. animals 3. crude oil 4. petroleum 5. natural gas 6. coal B. 1. √ 3. √ 5. √ C. People can help make fossil fuel supplies last longer by driving their cars less, using less electricity, and turning down the heat in their homes. They can also find other sources of energy to use, like sunlight and wind.

Lesson 5 How Do We Use Air?

Bring in large coffee cans and some white paper. Ask students to line the cans with paper. Smear the paper with petroleum jelly. Place the cans outside on a window ledge. After reading the lesson, bring in the cans. Carefully remove the paper linings and lay them out flat. Invite students to examine the dust and debris trapped by the jelly with a magnifying glass.

Answers page 83: A. 1. gases 2. air 3. gravity 4. air 5. plants 6. harmful gases 7. planting trees B. 1. Unhealthy 2. Healthy 3. Healthy 4. Unhealthy 5. Unhealthy C. Besides looking nice, plants remove carbon dioxide and add oxygen to the air in the house, making the air healthier.

Lesson 6 How Do We Use Water?

Arrange a visit to a water purification site or water source, or invite a water agency speaker to visit. Discuss the source of your town's or city's water supply. Help students understand that aquifers cannot supply an endless amount of water, so we need to keep streams and rivers unpolluted.

Answers page 85: A. 1. True 2. False 3. True 4. False 5. False B. 1. oceans 2. electricity 3. taking long showers 4. harmful materials 5. anything harmful C. A person can use less water to wash or bathe and to brush teeth.

Hands-On Activity *page 86* Students will engage in the process skill of making and using models as they practice a simple paper-making process. Provide students with needed materials. For each group, cut a 9-inch by 12-inch section of window screen. Place masking tape or electrician's tape along the sides to cover the sharp edges. The flat pan could be a large baking pan or a paint roller tray. Students should spread the newspaper mush as thinly and evenly as possible on the screen.

Answers: 1. The product is obviously paper; it can be folded, torn, and written on. It is rougher than ordinary paper, and is probably gray. 2. Making paper from old paper uses old paper that would otherwise be burned or go into a landfill. It also saves trees that would be cut down to be made into paper.

Blackline Masters for Chapter 5:
Problem Solving Skill, page 34; Chapter Review, page 42; Letter to Family (English/Spanish), page 60

"What Is It?" *Answer:* mineral

Chapter Test *page 87*
Answers: 1. A 2. D 3. C 4. B 5. A 6. B 7. C 8. D 9. C 10. B

After Reading the Chapter

Writing Ask students to contact their local utility company and find out which resources are used to supply energy to local customers. Then, ask students to prepare a display for a booth at an imaginary fair sponsored by the utility company. The students could work in groups to research, write, and illustrate explanations of present and alternative energy sources—wind, solar, nuclear, and water. Students should be sure to include the advantages and disadvantages of each energy source.

Chapter Summary Earth's atmosphere has five layers. Water evaporates, condenses into clouds, and falls in a continuous water cycle. The force of air, or air pressure, varies with altitude and temperature. Wind occurs when air moves from a high pressure area to a low pressure area. When air masses of different temperatures and pressures meet, they form a front. Meteorologists use sophisticated technology to measure, record, and forecast the weather.

Chapter Objectives Students will learn to
- recognize the five layers of Earth's atmosphere.
- explain Earth's water cycle.
- identify the relationship among air pressure, temperature, and wind.
- describe how air masses interact.
- understand how meteorologists measure and forecast the weather.

Vocabulary

troposphere, p. 90	sea level, p. 94
stratosphere, p. 90	expands, p. 94
mesosphere, p. 90	thermometers, p. 94
thermosphere, p. 90	barometers, p. 94
exosphere, p. 90	contracts, p. 96
altitudes, p. 90	air masses, p. 96
ozone, p. 90	tropical, p. 96
water cycle, p. 92	polar, p. 96
solar energy, p. 92	arctic, p. 96
molecules, p. 92	continental, p. 96
water vapor, p. 92	maritime, p. 96
evaporation, p. 92	anemometers, p. 96
humidity, p. 92	weather vane, p. 96
condensation, p. 92	forecast, p. 98
groundwater, p. 92	front, p. 98
runoff, p. 92	cold front, p. 98
meteorologists, p. 94	warm front, p. 98
air pressure, p. 94	stationary front, p. 98
hurricane, p. 100	radar, p. 100
tornado, p. 100	weather stations, p. 100
satellites, p. 100	

Vocabulary Activity Have pairs of students write a script for a television weather report using the vocabulary words. When students complete the last lesson, ask them to create original weather maps to use as backdrops for weather reports they present to the class.

Before Reading the Chapter Ask students to volunteer answers to the "What Is It?" riddle in the Chapter Opener. Then, talk with students about the effects of weather on their daily lives.

Lesson 1 What Are the Layers in the Atmosphere?
As students read, be sure they understand that every layer in the atmosphere is important. The layers that blanket Earth protect it from the sun's radiation and keep its temperature moderate and stable.
Answers page 91: A. 1. atmosphere 2. troposphere 3. warmer than 4. exosphere 5. troposphere B. 1. True 2. False 3. True 4. True 5. False C. The troposphere affects human beings the most. It contains about 75 percent of all the air in the atmosphere, and about 99 percent of all the water vapor in the air. The weather changes that we feel on the ground take place in the troposphere.

Lesson 2 How Do Clouds and Rain Form?
Point out that water vapor is not visible. Breathe softly on a mirror and show students how vapor in your breath condenses on the mirror's surface.
Answers page 93: A. 1. molecules 2. high 3. water vapor 4. liquid water 5. runoff B. 1. evaporation—the change from liquid water to water vapor 2. humidity—the amount of water vapor in the air 3. condensation—the change from water vapor to liquid water 4. precipitation—water that falls from clouds 5. groundwater—water beneath Earth's surface C. No, the water cycle is always repeating. It is not possible to say where it starts or ends.

Lesson 3 What Is Air Pressure?

Demonstrate that air exerts pressure in all directions. Tie strings to the corners of a cloth handkerchief to create a simple parachute. Attach a paper clip to the loose ends of all four strings. Drop the parachute and ask students to explain why it opens and falls slowly. (Air from below pushes up on the parachute.)

Answers page 95: A. 1. air pressure 2. pounds 3. temperature 4. into 5. temperature 6. air pressure B. 1. Meteorologists are people who study the weather. 2. Air pressure is the weight of air pressing on Earth. 3. Thermometers are used to measure temperature. 4. Fahrenheit is one scale for measuring temperature. C. Students should answer that they would expect the air pressure to be high because cool air is thicker.

Lesson 4 What Makes the Wind Blow?

Demonstrate that warm air expands using a medium balloon, hot water, and a narrow-necked bottle. Fill the bottle with hot water and set it aside for a minute. Pour the water out and immediately fit the balloon securely over the bottle neck. The warm air in the bottle expands to inflate the balloon. When you remove the balloon, air escapes, creating wind.

Answers page 97: A. 1. True 2. True 3. False 4. True 5. False B. 1. winds 2. air mass 3. tropical 4. continental 5. maritime C. Maritime air masses probably come from over the sea, where they have picked up their high humidity.

Lesson 5 What Are Fronts?

Invite a meteorologist to speak to the class. If possible, show students a video on thunderstorms and other severe weather conditions.

Answers page 99: A. 1. front 2. forecast 3. beneath 4. over 5. stationary B. 1. cold front moves in—weather becomes stormy 2. warm front moves in—light, steady precipitation starts 3. stationary front forms—long period of mild weather 4. cold front passes by—weather turns cooler C. Weather satellites make it possible to collect information over larger areas, such as the oceans.

Lesson 6 How Do People Predict Weather?

Bring in recent reports from a newspaper weather page. Invite students to examine the weather maps and decipher the signs and symbols.

Encourage students to create original weather maps for their chapter vocabulary activity.

Answers page 101: A. 1. data 2. equipment 3. satellites 4. radio waves 5. symbols B. 1. False 2. False 3. True 4. True C. Answers will vary, but students might mention using weather reports to learn if the weather will be good for future outdoor activities.

Hands-On Activity *page 102* Students will engage in the process of modeling as they make a simple wind speed indicator. Provide students with needed materials. Foam balls should be 2–3 inches in diameter. If students have trouble getting the tape to stick to the foam ball, try wrapping the string around the point of a thumbtack and pressing it into the foam ball. If students are unable to go outside, bring a variable-speed electric fan into the classroom and do the activity there. Make sure students mark their indicators at equal intervals. The particular size of the intervals does not matter.

Answers: 1. Answers will vary. Students may say that the lowest wind speed they recorded was 0; the highest was a little over 3. 2. Answers will vary. Accept all reasonable answers.

Blackline Masters for Chapter 6:

Problem Solving Skill, page 35; Chapter Review, page 43; Letter to Family (English/Spanish), page 61

"What Is It?" *Answer:* front

Chapter Test *page 103*

Answers: 1. A 2. A 3. B 4. A 5. C 6. C 7. D 8. D 9. A 10. B

After Reading the Chapter

Writing Explain how analogies can be used to extend meaning. Ask students to select several vocabulary words and make a list of all the things, feelings, sounds, and sights that the words bring to mind. Then, ask the students to write about weather using analogies. For example, to describe a very hot day, students might say: The mercury climbed up the thermometer like an athlete sprinting to the finish line.

Unit Summary Energy comes in many forms—heat energy, light energy, mechanical energy, and electrical energy. The electromagnetic spectrum includes radio waves, infrared radiation, visible light, ultraviolet light, X rays, and gamma rays. Energy creates force to do work. Work is done when a force moves an object in the same direction as the direction of the force. Simple machines like the lever, wheel and axle, pulley, inclined plane, screw, and wedge, make work easier.

Before Reading the Unit Ask students to describe the differences between daily life a hundred years ago and daily life today. Ask them to explain how discoveries about energy have affected our lives. Ask how the inventions of tools and machines have changed our lifestyles over time. Then invite students to look at the diagrams and illustrations in Chapters 7 and 8. Tell students that Unit 3 presents information about energy sources. It also presents information about how work is made easier with simple machines.

Unit Performance Project

Setup and Presentation Page 54 in this Teacher's Guide contains a reproducible project that focuses on the use of energy and simple machines to do work. Present the project after you have studied how energy moves and the uses of simple machines. (Chapters 7 and 8)

Evaluation A satisfactory project should show a basic sketch for a device that uses two forms of energy—such as heat energy for fuel and mechanical energy—and at least two parts that are simple machines. It should also include a basic description of how the machine works.

A good project should show more details and complete explanations of how the device works.

An outstanding project should also show every detail of the machine, with very clear explanations of how it works and how it uses energy. There is a rubric on page 55 in this Teacher's Guide that will assist students in evaluating their work.

Careers Feature

Page 138 of the student text offers students a glimpse into the careers of a recording engineer, auto mechanic, and mechanical engineer. Explain that people who enter these fields generally complete a course of study in a technical school or college. Some may also receive on-the-job training, for example, in a recording studio or in an automobile repair shop. Ask students what kinds of special skills and interests people in each field might need. Point out that some people have aptitudes for working with tools and for complicated mathematics. People who work as recording engineers generally also have an interest in music and sound. Ask if students might be interested in entering any of these fields. Suggest that students choose one of the fields to research. Have them read articles on the Internet or in periodicals to learn about recent developments in the field. They may also want to visit a recording studio or mechanic's shop to learn more about the professions. Ask them to write brief reports on what they have learned.

Unit Test The Blackline Master for Unit 3 Test is on page 48 of the Teacher's Guide. The test is in the standardized test format to provide students with practice in taking standardized tests. The unit test content focuses on the movement of energy, the names for different types of energy, and how simple machines make work easier.

Answers: 1. B 2. C 3. B 4. A 5. C 6. D 7. D 8. A 9. A 10. C

After Reading the Unit Point out to students that this unit contains practical information they can use in everyday situations. Ask: How does the information help you understand how machines and energy work? Might it change the way you use energy in your daily lives? How might these lessons help you plan ahead when you are completing a project that involves heavy labor? How might information from this unit help an engineer plan and design machines that save energy?

Chapter Summary There are many kinds of energy, and energy can change forms. Forms of energy include heat energy, sound energy, light energy, mechanical energy, and electrical energy. The sun provides heat and light energy. Electromagnetic waves include radio waves, infrared radiation, visible light, ultraviolet light, X rays, and gamma rays.

Chapter Objectives Students will learn to
- define *temperature* and *heat.*
- explain conduction, convection, and radiation.
- describe light energy, sound energy, mechanical energy, and electricity.
- explain how energy changes forms.
- describe the importance of the sun.
- interpret the electromagnetic spectrum.

Vocabulary

temperature, p. 108	potential energy, p. 114
heat, p. 108	
molecules, p. 108	solar heaters, p. 116
conduction, p. 110	electromagnetic radiation, p. 118
convection, p. 110	
radiation, p. 110	electromagnetic spectrum, p. 118
light energy, p. 112	
sound energy, p. 112	radio waves, p. 118
mechanical energy, p. 112	microwaves, p. 118
electrical energy, p. 112	infrared radiation, p. 118
turbine, p. 114	visible light, p. 118
generator, p. 114	ultraviolet light, p. 118
kinetic energy, p. 114	X rays, p. 118
	gamma rays, p. 118

Vocabulary Activity Ask students to create a comic strip character to introduce energy to younger students. Then, as students read the chapter, have them create a comic book that explains the vocabulary words in pictures and words that younger students can understand.

Before Reading the Chapter Ask students to answer the "What Is It?" riddle in the Chapter Opener. Then initiate a discussion about sources of energy. Ask students what kinds of energy they can feel or see, and what kinds of energy are invisible.

Lesson 1 What Are Temperature and Heat?
Hang a plastic bag of water in full sunlight or near a window. Several hours later, pour the contents of the bag into a bowl and invite students to feel the temperature of the water. Ask students to explain how the water became warm. (Heat energy from the sun radiated through empty space to heat the water.)

Answers page 109: A. 1. True 2. False 3. False 4. True 5. True B. 1. higher temperature 2. lower temperature 3. higher temperature 4. lower temperature 5. lower temperature 6. higher temperature C. The molecules in the cold butter move slowly. When the butter is placed in the hot pan, heat energy from the pan moves into the butter. The butter molecules move faster and the butter melts.

Lesson 2 How Does Heat Move?
Ask students to talk about their experiences with cooking. Ask them what happens when water boils or why some pot handles become hot and others don't.

Answers page 111: A. 1. conduction 2. conduction 3. convection 4. radiation 5. radiation 6. conduction B. cup of liquid—conduction (heat moving from liquid into cup; also heat moving from liquid into air over cup); heat lamps—radiation (heat moving through space down from lamps to food); boiling water—convection (heated water at bottom of pot moving up to top, and cooler water moving down to take its place) C. The air in the room gets heated by convection, and the air transfers heat to objects in the room by conduction. Heat also radiates from the heater to objects in the room.

Lesson 3 What Are Other Forms of Energy?
Bring in two metal forks and a 3-foot length of cotton string. Tie a fork to the string and let it hang down while you hold the other end of the string. Hit the fork with the other fork, and

listen to it ring. Then invite students to hold the loose end of string against their heads and listen again when the fork is rung. Ask students what happens and why. (The ringing is clear and loud. Sound waves travel easily along the string and vibrate the listener's skull.)

Answers page 113: A. 1. light 2. sound 3. sound waves 4. mechanical 5. electrical B. 1. Light energy is produced by the sun and other stars. 2. Heat energy and light energy travel through empty space. 3. Sound energy travels in waves through the air. 4. Mechanical energy is the energy of moving objects. 5. Electrical energy flows through wires to run lights and motors. C. Sound energy is a type of mechanical energy. To travel, it needs the motion of some material such as air molecules. Empty space contains no material, so sound cannot travel in empty space.

Lesson 4 Can Energy Change Forms?
Ask an auto mechanic to show the class a car engine and to explain how an internal combustion engine works and how burning fossil fuel creates heat and pressure to drive pistons, creating mechanical energy to spin the wheels.

Answers page 115: A. 1. potential energy 2. kinetic energy 3. potential energy 4. potential energy 5. kinetic energy 6. kinetic energy B. heat energy, mechanical energy, electrical energy C. When the toy is wound up, the spring inside it has energy stored in it. This is potential energy. When the toy is started, the potential energy turns into the energy of motion. This is kinetic energy.

Lesson 5 Where Does Our Energy Come From?
Ask students to list machines or tools they use that require energy. Ask them to create sequence charts that trace the energy back to its source. For example, a car's mechanical energy (3) is fueled by fossil fuels (2) that contain energy once received by plants from the sun (1).

Answers page 117: A. 1. True 2. True 3. False 4. True 5. False 6. False B. light energy, food, sun C. Cars run on gasoline, which is a fossil fuel. So the energy in gasoline comes from the sun.

Lesson 6 What Is the Electromagnetic Spectrum?
Be sure students understand that electromagnetic waves are energy waves of different lengths that can pass through empty space.

Scientists have given them different names to differentiate between the ways we perceive them. For example, we can see visible light waves, transmit sound on radio waves, and feel heat from infrared waves.

Answers page 119: A. 1. electromagnetic radiation 2. electromagnetic spectrum 3. radio waves 4. visible light 5. X rays and gamma rays B. 1. Radio waves are used to broadcast television programs. 2. Microwaves can be used to cook food. 3. Infrared radiation is another name for heat energy. 4. Ultraviolet light causes sunburn. 5. X rays are used by doctors. C. Answers will vary.

Hands-On Activity *page 120* Students will practice the process skill of observing as they experiment with convection currents in water. Provide students with needed materials. The tall cups should be clear, and the droppers should reach the bottom of the cups. Safety tip: Hot tap water should be used for this activity. It should be about the temperature of bath water.

Answers: 1. The colored water stayed at the bottom of the glass because it was the same temperature as the water that surrounded it. 2. The colored water rose to the top of the glass because it was warmer than the water that surrounded it. 3. Answers will vary. Accept all reasonable answers.

Blackline Masters for Chapter 7:
Problem Solving Skill, page 36; Chapter Review, page 44; Letter to Family (English/Spanish), page 62

"What Is It?" *Answer:* sound

Chapter Test *page 121*
Answers: 1. B 2. A 3. D 4. B 5. C 6. C 7. D 8. A 9. A 10. B

After Reading the Chapter
Writing Read a science fiction story to students. Invite students to write original science fiction stories in which aliens can perceive more of the electromagnetic spectrum than we can. Encourage students to support their stories with factual information.

Chapter Summary Work is done when force pushes an object and makes it change positions. Simple machines make work easier. The lever is a simple machine that pivots on a fulcrum and increases force. A wheel and axle reduces friction to make work easier. Pulleys change the direction of the force, making it easier for people to lift heavy objects. Other simple machines include the inclined plane, the screw, and the wedge.

Chapter Objectives Students will learn to
- explain *force.*
- define *friction* and *work.*
- understand how levers, a wheel and axle, and pulleys work.
- demonstrate how an inclined plane, a screw, and a wedge work.

Vocabulary

force, p. 124	load, p. 128
friction, p. 126	wheel and axle, p. 130
work, p. 126	pulley, p. 132
machine, p. 128	inclined plane, p. 134
simple machine, p. 128	screw, p. 134
lever, p. 128	wedge, p. 134
fulcrum, p. 128	

Vocabulary Activity Assign partners one vocabulary word each to define for the class. Encourage students to draw diagrams or to perform a demonstration to help other students understand the word.

Before Reading the Chapter Ask students to answer the "What Is It?" riddle in the Chapter Opener. Assemble a classroom collection of common hand tools, including a hammer and nails, a screwdriver and screws, and a rope and pulley. Also bring in two blocks of soft wood. Ask students to talk about hand tools they have used and have them explain how each tool helped them complete a job. Encourage them to

mention everyday activities that would be impossible without simple tools. (for example, cutting your hair, opening a bottle)

Lesson 1 What Is Force?
Demonstrate force by pushing a book across a desk. Discuss how the amount of force to move a book differs from the amount of force needed to propel a large object like a jet plane. Ask students to explain how much force is required for each movement, and help them understand the relationship between the amount of force expended and the resulting amount of energy.
Answers page 125: A. 1. force 2. position 3. energy 4. direction 5. gravity 6. strong B. 1. True 2. False 3. False 4. False 5. True C. Even though the building may be large, it is still small compared to huge objects like Earth. So the building's gravity is too weak to have any effect on a person standing near it.

Lesson 2 How Does Force Affect Motion?
Ask students to rub their hands together while pressing hard. Ask if students can explain why it is difficult for their hands to move. Explain that friction makes some tasks harder.
Answers page 127: A. 1. friction 2. friction 3. work 4. friction B. 1. force 2. gravity 3. work 4. gravity 5. friction C. Gravity does work by applying a force to move an object in the same direction as the pull of gravity. A ball dropping is an example of work done by gravity.

Lesson 3 What Is a Lever?
Assemble a hammer, nails, and a block of soft wood. Help students observe how a hammer functions as a lever. Demonstrate pounding nails halfway into the wood. Ask students to identify the fulcrum and the direction of force. Then show students how to pull out the nails, using the claw end of the hammer as a lever. Again, encourage them to observe the location of the fulcrum and the direction of force.
Answers page 129: A. 1. True 2. False 3. True 4. True 5. True 6. True 7. True 8. True B. 1. A playground seesaw is a lever with the fulcrum in the center. 2. A bottle opener is a lever with the fulcrum at the same end as the load. 3. A

hammer is a lever with the fulcrum at the end opposite the load. C. When the friends climb onto the seesaw, their weight pushes down on their end. This is the force. Your end of the seesaw rises into the air. You are the load. The seesaw is a lever with the fulcrum in the center.

Lesson 4   What Is a Wheel and Axle?
Students may want to look at the mechanics of a bicycle and discuss how much energy is saved by the wheel and axle system. Ask students to measure the circumference of the bicycle tire and the circumference of the axle. Have them calculate how much greater a distance the tire travels than the axle. Explain that the pedals are like points on an invisible wheel attached to a much narrower axle. Turning the pedals requires less force than turning the axle.

Answers page 131: A. 1. simple machine 2. wheel and axle 3. wheel 4. axle 5. work 6. circle 7. smaller and stronger B. 1. reduce 2. increase 3. do not change C. The larger part of the doorknob, the knob, is the wheel. The axle is the thinner part that goes inside the door. The knob makes the axle easier to turn.

Lesson 5   What Is a Pulley?
Bring in three pulleys, a good length of cord, and several books bound together. Invite groups of students to take turns rigging up efficient systems for lifting the books to the top of a table or a shelf.

Answers page 133: A. 1. True 2. False 3. False 4. False 5. False B. 1. direction 2. two pulleys 3. many pulleys C. 1. A single pulley does not increase force. 2. A double pulley increases force. 3. A block and tackle increases force. D. A 100-pound force can lift a 200-pound object because a double pulley doubles the force.

Lesson 6   What Is an Inclined Plane?
Talk about how we use simple machines in everyday life. Ask students to describe ways they and other people use inclined planes, screws, and wedges to help with difficult tasks. Ask them how they use simple machines when playing sports.

Answers page 135: A. 1. an inclined plane 2. an inclined plane 3. a screw 4. a screw 5. a wedge 6. a wedge B. 1. jar lid 2. knife 3. parking garage ramp C. Teeth are tiny wedges used to split food into smaller pieces.

Hands-On Activity *page 136* Students will practice the process skills of experimenting and observing as they test how friction affects a sliding object. Explain that the wood block will eventually slide off of the book as the book becomes an inclined plane. Students will test how different surfaces increase or decrease friction. Provide students with needed materials. For Step 6 you may want to provide extra materials for students to test, such as cloth towels, wax paper, or tissue paper.

Answers: 1. Answers will vary. Students might mention that the sandpaper created the most friction. 2. Answers will vary. Students might mention that the aluminum foil created the least friction. If students rubbed the wood block with soap, friction would be reduced further.

Blackline Masters for Chapter 8:
Problem Solving Skills, page 37; Chapter Review, page 45; Letter to Family (English/Spanish), page 63

"What Is It?" *Answer:* simple machine

Chapter Test *page 136*
   Answers: 1. C 2. B 3. A 4. A 5. B 6. C 7. A 8. D 9. B 10. D

After Reading the Chapter
Mathematics Help students create mathematical equations that describe ratios using pulley systems. For example, students can determine the ratio of rope length to the amount of weight it can lift. Using pulleys, they can double or triple the weight load to check their equations. They can also determine the ratio of work done by one, two, and three pulleys.
Social Studies Divide the class into six groups. Have each group research the history of one simple machine. Ask them to determine when and where the tool was probably invented, and how people have used the tool since its invention. Ask students to present their research to the class. Encourage them to use visual aids.

Name _____   Date _____

Problem Solving Skill

Making Inferences

These pictures show the same wildflower patch four summers in a row.

Three Years Ago	Two Years Ago

Last Year	This Year

1. Look at the first three pictures. How did the wildflower patch change? Why do you think these changes happened?

   _____

   _____

   _____

2. How does the wildflower patch in the last picture look different from the wildflower patch in earlier summers? What do you think were some possible reasons for this change?

   _____

   _____

   _____

© Harcourt Achieve Inc. All rights reserved. *Focus on Science Level E*

Name _____   Date _____

Problem Solving Skill

Drawing Conclusions

Look at the picture of the lake site. Look for evidence of animal life. Identify each clue as a bird, a fish, a mammal, an insect, an amphibian, or a reptile. Write your answers on the drawings.

Name _____   Date _____

Problem Solving Skill

Measuring and Recording Data

Two important signs of a person's physical health are the heartbeat and breathing rate. These can be measured easily. Find your heartbeat, or pulse,

by placing the first two fingers of one hand gently on the front of the other wrist. (Do not use your thumb because it has a pulse also.) Use a watch and count the number of heartbeats in one minute. You might want to have a partner observe the time. Measure your breathing rate by counting the number of times you take a breath in one minute. Try to breathe naturally.

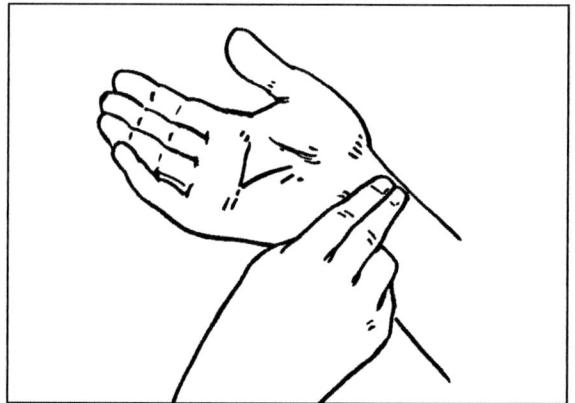

Imagine that you want a job in a fitness center during your summer vacation. Before you can have the job, the center has asked you to test your own personal fitness by measuring your heart and breathing rates. Begin by taking your pulse and breathing rate in a state of rest (sitting down). Then do 20 jumping jacks. When you stop, immediately measure your pulse and breathing rates. Then, measure again five minutes later. Record your results on the chart below. When you are rested, run in place for 2 minutes and take your pulse and breathing rate in the same way.

Name _____	Pulse	Breathing Rate
At rest	_____	_____
After 20 jumping jacks		
• immediately after	_____	_____
• 5 minutes later	_____	_____
After running in place for 2 minutes		
• immediately after	_____	_____
• 5 minutes later	_____	_____

   © Harcourt Achieve Inc. All rights reserved. *Focus on Science Level E*

Problem Solving Skill

Interpreting a Biome Map

You are a wildlife photographer. You want to photograph each animal listed below in its natural home. Look at the map. Which biome would you visit to see each animal? Explain your choice.

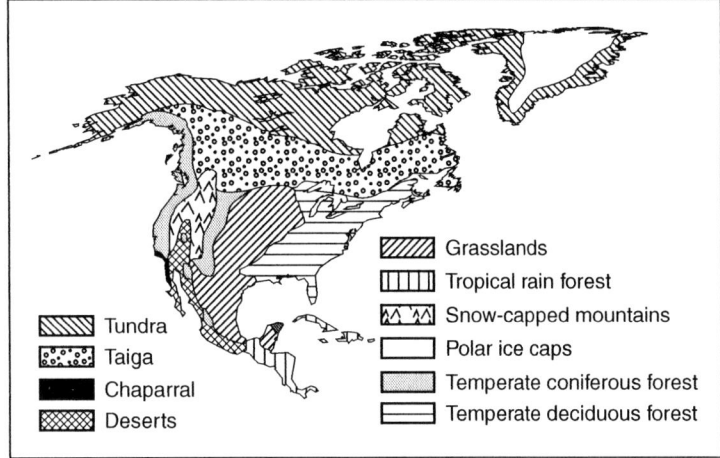

Tundra
Taiga
Chaparral
Deserts

Grasslands
Tropical rain forest
Snow-capped mountains
Polar ice caps
Temperate coniferous forest
Temperate deciduous forest

1. The *Polar Bear* lives in a snow den for four months each year. Here, she gives birth to cubs and nurses them. She hunts seals by jumping from iceberg to iceberg.

1. _____
_____
_____
_____

2. The *Western Harvest Mouse* feeds on seeds, grass, and insects. It builds round nests of grass, and feeds mainly at night to avoid predators.

2. _____
_____
_____
_____

3. The *Fruit Bat* flies from plant to plant to pollinate and feed. These bats roost in groups in large hollow trees, and in the leaves of palm trees. They feed on fruit like bananas, figs, and guava.

3. _____
_____
_____
_____

4. The *Moose* is a good swimmer. It eats young deciduous trees and plants that grow in shallow water.

4. _____
_____
_____
_____

Name _____   Date _____

Problem Solving Skill

Gathering and Interpreting Data

Most of Earth's surface is covered with water. More than 97% of the water is ocean water. About 2% of the water is freshwater that is frozen in ice caps and glaciers. Only 1% of the water is freshwater that is not frozen. Freshwater is stored in the atmosphere and in lakes, rivers, and underground lakes, called *aquifers*. Every living thing on Earth needs clean freshwater.

Water is called a renewable resource. As Earth becomes more crowded, we need to be sure our water supply will last. Already, pollution and overuse threaten it. People pump water from aquifers. Sometimes people bury toxic wastes near aquifers, or dump chemicals into rivers or lakes. And sometimes people use more water than they need.

1. On the back of this paper or on a separate sheet of paper, draw two large clocks, one for A.M. and one for P.M. Use the clocks below as models for your large clocks. Mark the hours on each clock, but do not include hands. Think about the ways you use water every day. On your large clocks, record how your family uses water at different times of the day.

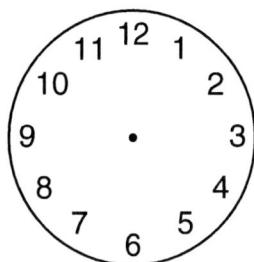

A.M.   P.M.

2. Think about the importance of water. In the future, how do you think people can protect and restore the freshwater supply?

_____

_____

_____

_____

   © Harcourt Achieve Inc. All rights reserved. *Focus on Science Level E*

Name _____ Date _____

Problem Solving Skill

Drawing Conclusions

Acid rain forms when chemicals from cars, factories, and power plants go into the atmosphere. The chemicals sulfur and nitrogen join with oxygen to form harmful gases. These gases mix with water vapor in the air. When the water vapor condenses, it falls to Earth as acid rain. Acid rain poisons plants and animals and can kill forests, lakes, and rivers.

| 30 Years Ago | 15 Years Ago | Today |

1. Lily Lake is 100 miles north of a big city. How has Lily Lake changed over the years? What do you think has caused these changes? How would you explain the changes to someone who has never visited Lily Lake?

_____

_____

_____

_____

2. How might people help bring back the trees and animals to Lily Lake?

_____

_____

_____

_____

© Harcourt Achieve Inc. All rights reserved. *Focus on Science Level E*

Problem Solving Skill

Judging and Evaluating

Radio waves are energy waves. They have different lengths, or frequencies. Radio waves can carry sounds great distances. People use radio waves to carry radio programs and to relay conversations on cellular phones. Satellites orbiting Earth use radio waves to send signals.

Astronomers and phone companies argue over the rights to certain radio frequencies. The astronomers say they can listen to these frequencies and hear pulses from distant points in the universe. They can use the pulses to get a picture of the universe. Phone companies say that people need to use the frequencies for communication. These frequencies help people around the world talk to one another.

As the world gets more crowded, people have different ideas about how to use these forms of energy. You be the judge. Who do you think should use these air waves? Why? How do you think this problem could be solved?

_____

_____

_____

_____

_____

_____

_____

_____

_____

_____

_____

_____

© Harcourt Achieve Inc. All rights reserved. *Focus on Science Level E*

Name _____ Date _____

Problem Solving Skill

Applying Information to New Situations

You are on a summer dig at an archaeological site. You have discovered the site of an ancient city, but before you can dig, you must remove two large boulders. They are too heavy to push, so you must build a simple machine. You are far from town. You can use only the materials near the site. Write a plan to solve the problem and remove the boulders. If you need to, draw a picture of your plan to help your work crew understand it.

_____

_____

_____

_____

_____

_____

_____

_____

_____

_____

© Harcourt Achieve Inc. All rights reserved. *Focus on Science Level E*

Name _____ Date _____

Chapter Review

Each of the following paragraphs tells about something you read in Chapter 1. Read each paragraph. Underline the word that makes each sentence correct.

The first plants on Earth were very different from those we see today. Scientists who study the earliest plants are called **(paleobotanists, paleogeologists)**. They learn about these plants by studying **(green algae, fossils)**. The first plants used photosynthesis to create food from sunlight. These plants came from earlier plant forms, known as **(green algae, fossils)**.

The first land plants appeared about 430 million years ago. They lived near water and lay flat on top of the damp mud. Millions of years later, vascular plants appeared. These plants have special tissues called **(xylem, ferns)** and phloem. These tissues carry water and nutrients throughout the plant. Vascular plants were able to stand up. Eventually, they covered Earth.

About 100 million years ago, flowering plants first appeared. Many flowering plants need insects to help them **(reproduce, grow)**. Insects carry **(water, pollen)** from plant to plant on their bodies.

Plants and animals have changed together over time. They are the two great partners in life on Earth. Plants provide animals with **(food, offspring)**. Animals help plants as well. People have changed plants. They have developed **(hybrid, domesticated)** plants by separating plants from their wild ancestors. They have also grown **(hybrid, domesticated)** plants by joining two species to make new plants.

 © Harcourt Achieve Inc. All rights reserved. *Focus on Science Level E*

Chapter Review

Each of the following paragraphs tells about something you read in Chapter 2. Read each paragraph. Underline the word that makes each sentence correct.

The first animals appeared about 600 million years ago. They were **(soft-bodied, hard-bodied)** creatures. Over millions of years, these animals developed hard coverings. Mollusks and trilobites are two examples.

Fish were the first **(vertebrates, invertebrates)**, or animals with backbones. The first fish had no **(mouths, jaws)**. The two main groups of fish had skeletons made mostly of bone or of **(cartilage, vertebrates)**.

The most successful of all animals are **(amphibians, insects)**. The first vertebrates to live out of the water were **(amphibians, reptiles)**. They are animals that live part of their lives in the water and part on land.

Animals that have dry, scaly skin are called **(amphibians, reptiles)**. They were the first vertebrates to live entirely on land. About 200 million years ago, two new forms of reptiles developed. One form was the crocodile. The other new reptiles were pterosaurs, which could **(fly, swim)**.

Dinosaurs ruled Earth for more than 140 million years. About 65 million years ago, dinosaurs suddenly became **(plentiful, extinct)**. Birds are feathered animals with wings. They developed from **(reptiles, mammals)**.

Mammals became widespread after **(dinosaurs, reptiles)** disappeared. This began to happen about 65 million years ago. Over millions of years, Earth has changed in many ways and is still changing. Animals that cannot **(swim, adapt)** will not survive.

© Harcourt Achieve Inc. All rights reserved. *Focus on Science Level E*

Chapter Review

Each of the following paragraphs tells about something you read in Chapter 3. Read each paragraph. Underline the word or words that make each sentence correct.

There are many systems that make our bodies work. One system is the **(digestive, skeletal)** system, which supports the body. It is made of bones and **(muscles, platelets)**.

Blood is made of plasma, red blood cells, and white blood cells. Red blood cells carry **(oxygen, carbon dioxide)** to all parts of the body and pick up **(oxygen, carbon dioxide)**, a waste gas. Platelets in the blood allow it to **(flow smoothly, clot)**.

The circulatory system moves blood around the body. The heart is the special muscle that pumps the blood. Blood that contains oxygen flows through **(veins, arteries)**. Blood that contains carbon dioxide flows through **(veins, arteries)**.

Breathing takes place in the respiratory system. This system includes the trachea, lungs, and **(diaphragm, esophagus)**. The exchange of oxygen and carbon dioxide takes place in the **(trachea, lungs)**.

The digestive system turns the food you eat into fuel. It includes the esophagus, stomach, and intestines. The stomach uses muscles and **(saliva, chemicals)** to break down food.

Your body cannot use all the material it takes in for food. Some of this material becomes waste. Waste is passed out of the body through the **(excretory, skeletal)** system. Three important parts of this system are the kidneys, lungs, and skin. Waste water and chemicals can leave the body through the skin when you **(breathe, sweat)**.

          © Harcourt Achieve Inc. All rights reserved. *Focus on Science Level E*

Name _____ Date _____

Chapter Review

Each of the following paragraphs tells about something you read in Chapter 4. Read each paragraph. Underline the word or words that make each sentence correct.

In every biome, different **(rainfall, deciduous)** patterns make life possible for certain plants. Different plants provide food and shelter for particular animals.

The tundra is a frozen land where only **(trees, grasses)** grow. The taiga is a **(warmer, colder)** biome than the tundra. Taiga evergreen trees provide homes to elk, bears, and moose.

Many living things have also adapted to the dry desert. Some animals feed after sunset. Cactus plants and some insects have waxy coatings that help them hold in water. To keep cool, camels store **(fat, water)** in humps on their backs.

A grassland biome gets **(more, less)** rain than a forest. In the grassland, it is hard for animals to hide from enemies. Some animals, like antelopes and gazelles, can move quickly. Smaller animals hide in underground **(burrows, herds)**.

In a deciduous forest, trees lose leaves each year. The wet, warm climate of a **(tropical rain, deciduous)** forest supports more kinds of life than any other biome. In the rain forest canopy, bats, snakes, and sloths climb and cling. African and South American rain forests have **(the same, different)** animals and plants.

Animals and plants have also adapted to life in aquatic biomes. Fish in marine biomes breathe **(saltwater, oxygen)** through gills. Tiny animals and plants called **(plankton, marine)** are a source of food for many fish.

© Harcourt Achieve Inc. All rights reserved. *Focus on Science Level E*

Name _____ Date _____

Chapter Review

Each of the following paragraphs tells about something you read in Chapter 5. Read each paragraph. Underline the word or words that make each sentence correct.

People use natural resources for food, clothing, shelter, and enjoyment. Renewable resources, such as air, trees, and water, can never be used up if they are **(polluted, protected)**.

Minerals are nonrenewable resources, mined from under the ground. Often, the mining process destroys plants that hold the soil. This soil can be **(replaced, lost)** when it erodes.

People protect soil from erosion by planting trees. Farmers replace nutrients in soil by adding **(compost, rocks)** and manure and by planting different crops.

Coal, petroleum, and natural gas are fossil fuels. Fossil fuels are created when, over millions of years, dead plants are pressed and heated deep inside Earth. Fossil fuels are a **(nonrenewable, renewable)** resource.

The Earth's atmosphere is made mostly of **(nitrogen, oxygen)**. Animals need oxygen to live, and plants need **(nitrogen, carbon dioxide)**. Earth is 75 percent water. Only **(three, thirty)** percent of that water is water that we can drink.

There are many ways people can protect natural resources. People can use **(less, more)** water every day. They can also use alternative sources of **(food, energy)** to preserve fossil fuels and keep the air clean.

 © Harcourt Achieve Inc. All rights reserved. *Focus on Science Level E*

Chapter Review

Each of the following paragraphs tells about something you read in Chapter 6. Read each paragraph. Underline the word or words that make each sentence correct.

Earth's atmosphere has five layers. The Space Shuttle has traveled through the exosphere. Planes fly in the **(stratosphere, mesosphere)**. The troposphere is the layer in which Earth's **(weather, temperature)** occurs.

During the water cycle, water is heated by solar energy and evaporates into invisible water vapor. When the vapor **(heats, cools)**, it condenses into frost and clouds. Heavy droplets in the clouds fall as precipitation. The water collects as groundwater or runoff to rivers, lakes, and the oceans.

Air pressure is all around us. Air pressure is created by **(humidity, gravity)**. When we are at sea level, pressure from the air above our heads is 14.7 pounds per square inch. At higher altitudes, air is **(lighter and thinner, heavier and thicker)**.

Warm air has a lower air pressure than cold air because warm air molecules move **(quickly, slowly)** and spread apart. When a tropical air mass and a polar air mass meet, the air from the **(polar, tropical)** mass moves to the low pressure area, causing wind.

When two air masses with **(similar, different)** properties meet, they form a front. Cold fronts **(rarely, often)** bring large changes in weather. Warm fronts usually bring **(light, heavy)**, steady precipitation

Meteorologists use **(barometers, anemometers)** to measure wind speed. They also use satellites to collect photographs and other data, and radar to track the movement and speed of storms.

Chapter Review

Each of the following paragraphs tells about something you read in Chapter 7. Read each paragraph. Underline the word or words that make each sentence correct.

Temperature is a measure of how hot or cold something is. Heat energy makes molecules move more **(slowly, quickly)**. This heat energy can move from one object to another.

When heat moves from a bowl of soup up the handle of a spoon, this movement is called **(convection, conduction)**. Heat can also move by radiating through **(empty space, plastic)**.

Light energy from the sun travels through empty space. Sound waves travel through the air and through **(objects, empty space)**. When a stick is carried downstream by a river, this is an example of **(mechanical, electrical)** energy.

Heat energy is used in a power plant to create **(mechanical, potential)** energy. By burning fossil fuels, water is heated to create steam. The steam turns a **(kinetic, turbine)**, which spins a generator, which changes heat energy into electrical energy.

The heat energy trapped in layers of our atmosphere comes from the **(electricity, sun)**. This energy is also known as infrared radiation. Some people use **(solar, potential)** energy for their homes. When fossil fuels burn, they release solar energy stored by plants millions of years ago.

Scientists call the energy waves radiated by the sun and other sources the electromagnetic **(properties, spectrum)**. These waves include radio waves, infrared radiation, visible light, ultraviolet light, X rays, and gamma rays. The light we can see makes up a **(tiny, large)** part of this spectrum.

© Harcourt Achieve Inc. All rights reserved. *Focus on Science Level E*

Chapter Review

Each of the following paragraphs tells about something you read in Chapter 8. Read each paragraph. Underline the word that makes each sentence correct.

A force is a push or pull that changes the **(position, mass)** of an object. All objects are pulled towards each other by the force of gravity. Work is done when you throw a ball into the air. Work is done when **(gravity, friction)** pulls the ball back down. When you roll a ball on the grass, **(incline, friction)** slows it down.

Simple machines like the lever make work easier for us. When we pry open a can of paint with a screwdriver, the screwdriver acts as a lever. This kind of lever changes the direction and amount of force. A hammer also works as a lever, with the **(wedge, fulcrum)** at one end. This kind of lever changes only the **(amount, direction)** of force.

Wheels on a pair of skates make work easier because they reduce **(distance, friction)**. A wheel and axle are connected. When the axle turns, the wheel turns a greater **(distance, force)**.

Pulleys also make work easier. When people use a block and tackle, or a system of pulleys, they have to pull a rope a **(shorter, longer)** distance, but are able to lift a much heavier weight.

An inclined plane, a screw, and a wedge all make work easier. A screw and a **(wedge, screwdriver)** are both forms of the inclined plane. An ax is a wedge that changes the direction of the force from a downwards force to a **(sideways, upwards)** force.

© Harcourt Achieve Inc. All rights reserved. *Focus on Science Level E*

Name _____   Date _____

Unit Test

Darken the circle next to the correct answer.

1. The first plants on Earth lived only
   - Ⓐ in tall trees.
   - Ⓑ in damp soil.
   - Ⓒ in the water.
   - Ⓓ on land.

2. Insects help flowering plants to
   - Ⓐ reproduce.
   - Ⓑ make food.
   - Ⓒ get rid of wastes.
   - Ⓓ grow taller.

3. Why do plants and animals change together?
   - Ⓐ Animals need plants to help them reproduce.
   - Ⓑ Many animals need plants for food.
   - Ⓒ Animals don't like to eat different plants.
   - Ⓓ Plants respond to changes in animals.

4. Where did the first animals on Earth develop?
   - Ⓐ in the rain forests
   - Ⓑ in the oceans
   - Ⓒ on cool mountain tops
   - Ⓓ on desert plateaus

5. The first vertebrates to come from the water and live on land were
   - Ⓐ insects.
   - Ⓑ dinosaurs.
   - Ⓒ amphibians.
   - Ⓓ bacteria.

6. Birds developed from
   - Ⓐ bats.
   - Ⓑ reptiles.
   - Ⓒ flying insects.
   - Ⓓ flying fish.

7. Vertebrates that have hair on their bodies and feed their young with milk are
   - Ⓐ mammals.
   - Ⓑ reptiles.
   - Ⓒ pterosaurs.
   - Ⓓ amphibians.

8. Along with muscles, what makes movement of the human body possible?
   - Ⓐ the skin
   - Ⓑ the feet
   - Ⓒ the skeleton
   - Ⓓ involuntary tendons

9. Besides red and white blood cells, what else does blood contain?
   - Ⓐ plasma and platelets
   - Ⓑ bone marrow
   - Ⓒ capillaries
   - Ⓓ blood vessels

10. Which system brings oxygen into your body and takes carbon dioxide out?
    - Ⓐ the digestive system
    - Ⓑ the circulatory system
    - Ⓒ the excretory system
    - Ⓓ the respiratory system

© Harcourt Achieve Inc. All rights reserved. *Focus on Science Level E*

Unit Test

Darken the circle next to the correct answer.

1. The temperature and rainfall patterns of a biome form its
   - Ⓐ weather.
   - Ⓑ savanna.
   - Ⓒ precipitation.
   - Ⓓ climate.

2. Which biome is home to more kinds of plants and animals than any other biome?
   - Ⓐ tropical rain forest
   - Ⓑ desert
   - Ⓒ grassland
   - Ⓓ taiga

3. Marine biomes are found in
   - Ⓐ tropical rain forests.
   - Ⓑ freshwater swamps.
   - Ⓒ lakes, ponds, rivers, and streams.
   - Ⓓ oceans.

4. What can bad farming habits and careless handling of garbage do to soil?
   - Ⓐ fertilize it
   - Ⓑ pollute it
   - Ⓒ erode it
   - Ⓓ protect it

5. Which of the following are fossil fuels?
   - Ⓐ sunlight and wind
   - Ⓑ nuclear energy and wood
   - Ⓒ petroleum, natural gas, and coal
   - Ⓓ electricity, sunlight, and water

6. Much of the oxygen in the atmosphere comes from
   - Ⓐ cars and factories.
   - Ⓑ plants.
   - Ⓒ power plants.
   - Ⓓ animals.

7. Water is one of Earth's natural resources that is
   - Ⓐ renewable.
   - Ⓑ nonrenewable.
   - Ⓒ impossible to pollute.
   - Ⓓ impossible to keep clean and safe.

8. Clouds are formed by
   - Ⓐ pollution in the air.
   - Ⓑ thunder and lightning.
   - Ⓒ condensation of water vapor in the air.
   - Ⓓ smoke.

9. Wind is caused by
   - Ⓐ air moving from high pressure places to low pressure places.
   - Ⓑ water vapor that condenses.
   - Ⓒ clouds that form close to Earth.
   - Ⓓ high humidity that forms over cold areas.

10. A front is described by its
    - Ⓐ humidity.
    - Ⓑ location.
    - Ⓒ precipitation.
    - Ⓓ temperature.

© Harcourt Achieve Inc. All rights reserved. *Focus on Science Level E*

Unit Test

Darken the circle next to the correct answer.

1. As water heats up, the water molecules
   - Ⓐ move slower and slower.
   - Ⓑ move faster and faster.
   - Ⓒ move closer together.
   - Ⓓ stop moving.

2. Besides conduction, what are two other ways heat can move?
   - Ⓐ evaporation and condensation
   - Ⓑ precipitation and gamma rays
   - Ⓒ convection and radiation
   - Ⓓ microwaves and ultraviolet radiation

3. Sound energy travels
   - Ⓐ by radiation through empty space.
   - Ⓑ by vibration of air molecules.
   - Ⓒ through power lines and phone wires.
   - Ⓓ as microwaves.

4. The energy that is stored in objects that are not moving is
   - Ⓐ potential energy.
   - Ⓑ heat energy.
   - Ⓒ solar energy.
   - Ⓓ kinetic energy.

5. The energy you get by eating food comes from
   - Ⓐ the soil.
   - Ⓑ electricity.
   - Ⓒ the sun.
   - Ⓓ fossil fuels.

6. When a force is applied to move an object in the same direction as the force,
   - Ⓐ friction speeds up the object.
   - Ⓑ there is no friction.
   - Ⓒ no work is done.
   - Ⓓ work is done.

7. A simple machine does work
   - Ⓐ by decreasing a force.
   - Ⓑ with two or more movements.
   - Ⓒ by reducing the amount of work.
   - Ⓓ with only one movement.

8. What simple machine is a disk attached to a post?
   - Ⓐ a wheel and axle
   - Ⓑ a pulley
   - Ⓒ a rolling lever
   - Ⓓ a posted disk

9. A double pulley changes the direction of the force and
   - Ⓐ doubles the force.
   - Ⓑ doubles the load.
   - Ⓒ decreases the force.
   - Ⓓ does not change the force.

10. A simple machine that is a slope that makes it easier to lift an object is
    - Ⓐ a wheel and axle.
    - Ⓑ a pulley.
    - Ⓒ an inclined plane.
    - Ⓓ a block and tackle.

© Harcourt Achieve Inc. All rights reserved. *Focus on Science Level E*

Answer Key

Answers to Problem Solving Blackline Masters

Chapter 1

1. Each year there are more flowers and insects. The plants provide food for the insects. And the insects help the plants pollinate and spread new plants.
2. There are fewer flowers and insects than in previous years. This is probably because whatever the person sprayed on the flowers must have been poisonous and it killed many insects. Because there were fewer insects, the flowers did not reproduce as well.

Chapter 2

Students should observe the following: There is evidence of an amphibian (footprints) in the mud, a reptile under the rocks, a mammal in the hole, an insect in the grass, a bird in the bush, and a fish (skeleton) in the dry mud.

Chapter 3

Answers will vary from student to student. Pulse and breathing rate should increase after exercise and then decrease about 5 minutes later.

Chapter 4

1. The *Polar Bear* lives in the tundra and near the polar ice cap. It lives in the snow and ice.
2. The *Western Harvest Mouse* lives in grassland areas. It uses grass for food, building a nest, and hiding from predators.
3. The *Fruit Bat* lives in the tropical rain forest where fruit and roosting trees are available.
4. The *Moose* lives in northern forests, including the taiga and deciduous forests. It often grazes in streams and ponds.

Chapter 5

1. Students should record on their clocks the times they use water throughout the day to brush their teeth, wash clothes, water gardens, and so forth.
2. Students might suggest that businesses and communities keep water clean by not dumping into lakes and streams, and that they protect aquifers from pollution. Students might also suggest that people try to desalt ocean water.

Chapter 6

1. Sulfur and nitrogen from car exhaust and factory smoke mixed with the oxygen and moisture in the air. When the clouds carrying these pollutants moved over Lily Lake, it rained acid rain, and the trees and animals began to die. This happened slowly, as the acid rain continued to fall.

2. To bring back the trees and animals, people will have to improve the water quality in the lake and in the rain that falls on it. They will have to cut pollution from factories and cars. They might also plant new trees to help improve the air quality.

Chapter 7

Answers may vary. Students should write a logical argument defending their judgment. They may explain why the air waves are more important to astronomers or telephone companies, or they may decide they should be shared.

Chapter 8

Answers will vary. Students should draw a simple plan and describe it. Students' plans should include simple machines such as a lever, an inclined plane, or a wheel and axle.

Answers to Chapter Review Blackline Masters

Chapter 1
paleobotanists
fossils
green algae
xylem
reproduce
pollen
food
domesticated
hybrid

Chapter 2
soft-bodied
vertebrates
jaws
cartilage
insects
amphibians
reptiles
fly
extinct
reptiles
dinosaurs
adapt

Chapter 3
skeletal
muscles
oxygen
carbon dioxide
clot
arteries
veins
diaphragm
lungs
chemicals
excretory
sweat

Chapter 4
rainfall
grasses
warmer
fat
less
burrows
tropical rain
different
oxygen
plankton

Chapter 5
protected
lost
compost
nonrenewable
nitrogen
carbon dioxide
three
less
energy

Chapter 6
stratosphere
weather
cools
gravity
lighter and thinner
quickly
polar
different
often
light
anemometers

Chapter 7
quickly
conduction
empty space
objects
mechanical
mechanical
turbine
sun
solar
spectrum
tiny

Chapter 8
position
gravity
friction
fulcrum
amount
friction
distance
longer
wedge
sideways

Name _____   Date _____

Unit Performance Project

Changes Over Time

Use poster board or butcher block paper to make a picture time line that shows the changes in plants and animals over time. Begin with the first plants that lived in water more than one billion years ago. End with examples of the many kinds of plants and animals that live today.

Use this chart to plan your time line.

3.5 billion years ago	**1 billion years ago**	**600 million years ago**

500 million years ago	**400 million years ago**	**300 million years ago**

200 million years ago	**100 million years ago**	**Today**

© Harcourt Achieve Inc. All rights reserved. *Focus on Science Level E*

Unit Performance Project

The Formation of a Thunderstorm

Draw a diagram of a thunderstorm. Using pictures and captions, explain how the *water cycle, temperature, air pressure,* and *fronts* are involved in the making of a thunderstorm.

Explain how a thunderstorm helps to restore natural resources in a biome like the one in which you live.

_____

_____

_____

_____

Name _____ Date _____

Unit Performance Project

A Plan for a Labor-Saving Device

There are many things you do every day that you could do faster or better if you had a machine or device to help you. Draw plans for a machine or device that would be useful to you. Your design must:

- be practical.

- use at least two different forms of energy.

- use at least two parts that are simple machines.

- include an explanation of how the device works.

© Harcourt Achieve Inc. All rights reserved. *Focus on Science Level E*

FOCUS ON
SCIENCE™

Unit Performance Project Rubrics

Unit 1: Changes Over Time

An **Outstanding** project shows:

1—drawn examples of all the main groups of plants and animals.

2—examples placed in the correct places on the timeline.

3—labels and explanations for each example.

Outstanding = 3 out of the 3 criteria listed above

Good = 2 out of 3

Satisfactory = 1 out of 3

Unit 2: The Formation of a Thunderstorm

An **Outstanding** project shows:

1—how a thunderstorm forms, represented by drawings and an explanatory paragraph.

2—details of the water cycle and the interaction of cold and warm air masses.

3—detailed, accurate, and complete explanations, using both words and pictures.

Outstanding = 3 out of the 3 criteria listed above

Good = 2 out of 3

Satisfactory = 1 out of 3

Unit 3: A Plan for a Labor-Saving Device

An **Outstanding** project shows:

1—a design for a labor-saving device that uses two forms of energy and includes at least two parts that are simple machines.

2—explanations of how energy changes forms and how simple machines help the design.

3—detailed and complete drawings and explanations of how the machine works.

Outstanding = 3 out of the 3 criteria listed above

Good = 2 out of 3

Satisfactory = 1 out of 3

© Harcourt Achieve Inc. All rights reserved. *Focus on Science Level E*

FOCUS ON
SCIENCE™

_____
Date/Fecha

Dear Family:
Your child has begun studying Chapter 1, *Plants Over Time.* This chapter tells about the earliest plants and how plant life has changed over billions of years.
Look with your child at the diagrams and illustrations in this chapter. Ask him or her to discuss what you see. If possible, look at flowers near your home to find pollen.
Below is an activity that will support your child's study of this chapter.
Thank you for your interest and support.

Estimada familia:
Su hijo o hija ha comenzado a estudiar el Capítulo 1: *Plants Over Time.* Este capítulo presenta información sobre las primeras plantas y sobre cómo han cambiado las plantas a través de miles de millones de años.
Observe con su hijo o hija los diagramas y las ilustraciones del capítulo. Pídale que hable sobre lo que ven. Si es posible, también busquen flores cerca de su casa para observar el polen.
A continuación presentamos una actividad adicional que pueden completar juntos. Muchas gracias por su apoyo e interés.

Sincerely,/Atentamente,

_____

Observing the Vascular System in Plants

Use a white carnation or a piece of celery to observe with your child how water moves through plants. Fill a glass with red-colored water. Put the plant in the water and let it sit overnight. Then observe how the colored water has moved through the plant.

El sistema vascular de las plantas

Consiga un clavel blanco o un apio para observar con su hijo o hija cómo se mueve el agua por las plantas. Llene un vaso con agua a la que le haya añadido colorante rojo. Coloque la planta en el vaso y déjela allí una noche. A la mañana siguiente, pueden observar cómo ha corrido el agua teñida por la planta.

© Harcourt Achieve Inc. All rights reserved. *Focus on Science Level E*

_____

Date / Fecha

Dear Family:

Your child is now studying Chapter 2, _Animals Over Time,_ which covers the development of animals on Earth. Your child will learn about the first animals and when different types of animals developed, including fish, insects, amphibians, reptiles, dinosaurs, birds, and mammals.

You might like to read this chapter with your child. You can refer to the diagrams to begin discussions about the different types of animals.

Below is an activity that will support your child's study of this chapter.

Thank you for your interest and support.

Estimada familia:

Su hijo o hija ha comenzado a estudiar el Capítulo 2: _Animals Over Time._ Este capítulo trata sobre el desarollo de los animales en nuestro planeta. Su hijo o hija aprenderá sobre los primeros animales y los períodos de tiempo en que se desarollaron los diferentes tipos de animales (como los peces, los insectos, los anfibios, los reptiles, los dinosaurios, las aves y los mamíferos).

Pueden leer juntos el capítulo y referirse a los diagramas para iniciar conversaciones acerca de los distintos tipos de animales.

A continuación presentamos una actividad adicional que pueden completar juntos. Muchas gracias por su apoyo e interés.

Sincerely, / Atentamente,

_____

Drawing an Insect in Its Environment

Ask your child to choose an insect, such as a bee, an ant, a grasshopper, or a butterfly. Help your child learn about the type of environment in which this insect can live. Then have your child make a drawing of the insect in its environment.

Dibujo de un insecto en su medio ambiente

Pida a su hijo o hija que escoja un insecto, como una abeja, una hormiga, un saltamontes o una mariposa. Ayúdele a informarse sobre el medio ambiente en que vive ese insecto. Luego pídale que haga un dibujo del insecto en su entorno.

© Harcourt Achieve Inc. All rights reserved. _Focus on Science Level E_

FOCUS ON
SCIENCE™

_____
Date/Fecha

Dear Family:

Your child is now studying Chapter 3, _Body Systems._ Your child will learn about bones and muscles, blood, and the circulatory, respiratory, digestive, and excretory systems.

You can help reinforce your child's studies by reading the chapter together, focusing on how each body system must work well for us to be healthy.

Below is an activity that will support your child's study of this chapter.

Thank you for your interest and support.

Estimada familia:

Su hijo o hija ha comenzado a estudiar el Capítulo 3: _Body Sytems._ En el capítulo aprenderá sobre los huesos y los musculos, así como los sistemas circulatorio, respiratorio, digestivo y excretorio.

Pueden leer juntos el capítulo para repasar lo que su hijo o hija ha aprendido. Al leer el capítulo, haga énfasis en la importancia de que todos los sistemas del cuerpo funcionen bien para mantenerse con buena salud.

A continuación presentamos una actividad adicional que pueden completar juntos. Muchas gracias por su apoyo e interés.

Sincerely,/Atentamente,

_____

Seeing Muscles Work in Pairs

After reading Lesson 1, have your child bend one arm at the elbow and then extend that arm outward several times. With the other hand, ask your child to feel the action of the muscles at the front and back of the upper arm (the biceps and triceps). When the arm is bent, the biceps contract and the triceps relax. When the arm is extended, the biceps relax and the triceps contract.

Músculos que trabajan en pares

Después de leer la Lección 1, pida a su hijo o hija que doble un brazo y lo extienda varias veces. Pídale que ponga la otra mano en el brazo que está moviendo, para sentir la acción de los músculos superiores e inferiores del brazo (los bíceps y los tríceps). Cuando el brazo está doblado, los bíceps se contraen y los tríceps se relajan. Cuando el brazo está extendido, los bíceps se relajan y los tríceps se contraen.

© Harcourt Achieve Inc. All rights reserved. _Focus on Science Level E_

Date/Fecha

Dear Family:

We are now studying Chapter 4, *Biomes.* You can support our studies of Earth's climatic and geographical regions by reading the chapter with your child and by completing the activity below.

Thank you for your interest and support.

Estimada familia:

Su hijo o hija ha comenzado a estudiar el Capítulo 4: *Biomes.* Para apoyar nuestro estudio de las regiones climáticas y geográficas de la Tierra, pueden leer juntos el capítulo y hacer las actividades adicionales que presentamos a continuación.

Muchas gracias por su apoyo e interés.

Sincerely,/Atentamente,

A Trip to the Zoo

Visit a local zoo or nature center. Discover which biomes animals live in naturally and learn about how climate affects how they obtain food and shelter.

Una excursión al zoológico

Visite un zoológico o un parque natural. Averigüen en qué "biome", o medio ambiente natural, viven los animales y cómo los afecta el clima en su obtención de alimento y refugio.

© Harcourt Achieve Inc. All rights reserved. *Focus on Science Level E*

FOCUS ON
SCIENCE™

Date/Fecha

Dear Family:

We are studying Chapter 5, *Earth's Resources*. Your child will learn how people use and protect renewable and nonrenewable resources. Please support our study of resources by reading this chapter with your child. You may also want to complete the activity below.

Thank you for your interest and support.

Estimada familia:

Su hijo o hija ha comenzado a estudiar el Capítulo 5: *Earth's Resources*. En este capítulo, su hijo o hija aprenderá sobre cómo usamos y protegemos los recursos naturales renovables y los no renovables. Pueden leer juntos el capítulo para apoyar nuestros estudios de los recursos del planeta. También pueden completar juntos las actividades que presentamos a continuación.

Muchas gracias por su apoyo e interés.

Sincerely,/Atentamente,

Recycle at Home

Work with your child to reuse and recycle household materials. Together, make a list of the things you throw away most often. Encourage your child to organize a family recycling program. If you have a garden, create a compost pile for organic garbage.

Reciclaje en casa

Ayude a su hijo o hija a reusar y a reciclar materiales de la casa. Hagan juntos una lista de las cosas que tiran a la basura en su casa con más frecuencia. Pregúntele cuáles desperdicios se podrían reducir, reusar o reciclar. Anímele a organizar un programa de reciclaje familiar. Si tienen un jardín, pueden hacer abono con los desperdicios orgánicos.

© Harcourt Achieve Inc. All rights reserved. *Focus on Science Level E*

FOCUS ON
SCIENCE™

Date/Fecha

Dear Family:

We are now studying Chapter 6, *Weather.* Your child will learn how wind and weather form, and how meteorologists measure and forecast weather. Please read the chapter together and ask your child to explain new discoveries about weather.

The activity below will help make information on weather relevant to your child's life.

Thank you for your interest and support.

Estimada familia:

Su hijo o hija ha comenzado a estudiar el Capítulo 6: *Weather.* En este capítulo, su hijo o hija aprenderá cómo el viento y las condiciones atmosféricas se forman en la troposfera, y cómo los meteorólogos miden y hacen pronósticos del tiempo. Por favor, lean el capítulo juntos y pida a su hijo o hija que explique descubrimientos recientes sobre el clima. La actividad que presentamos a continuación servirá para que la información sobre el clima tenga más relevancia en la vida de su hijo o hija.

Muchas gracias por su apoyo e interés.

Sincerely,/Atentamente,

Take a Walk

Walk with your child, and ask your child to explain weather phenomena. Share observations about temperature, clouds, wind, and precipitation. Encourage your child to explain the water cycle, wind formation, air pressure, and temperature change.

Un paseo con el tiempo

Dé un paseo con su hijo o hija y pídale que le explique el fenómeno del clima. Conversen sobre la temperatura, las nubes, el viento y la precipitación. Anímele a explicar el ciclo de agua, la formación del viento, la presión atmosférica y los cambios de temperatura.

FOCUS ON
SCIENCE™

Date/Fecha

Dear Family:

We are studying Chapter 7, *How Energy Changes.* Your child will learn about different forms of energy, how energy changes, and where energy comes from. You might like to read this chapter with your child.

The activity below will also enrich our class study.

Thank you for your interest and support.

Estimada familia:

Su hijo o hija ha comenzado a estudiar el Capítulo 7: *How Energy Changes.* En este capítulo, su hijo o hija aprenderá sobre los diferentes tipos de energía, la manera en que cambia la energía y de dónde proviene. Pueden leer el capítulo juntos para repasar lo que ha aprendido en clase. La actividad que presentamos a continuación también enriquecerá el aprendizaje de su hijo o hija.

Muchas gracias por su apoyo e interés.

Sincerely,/Atentamente,

Observe Energy in the Kitchen

Cook a meal with your child. Talk with your child about energy exchange as you watch water coming to a boil, pots and utensils heating up, steam escaping, and frozen foods defrosting.

La energía en la cocina

Cocine una comida con su hijo o hija. Conversen sobre el intercambio de energía mientras observan el agua que comienza a hervir, las ollas y los utensilios que se comienzan a calentar, el vapor que se escapa y los alimentos congelados que se descongeln.

© Harcourt Achieve Inc. All rights reserved. *Focus on Science Level E*

FOCUS ON
SCIENCE™

Date/Fecha

Dear Family:

We are studying Chapter 8, *Simple Machines.* Your child will learn how force creates motion when people use levers, wheels and axles, pulleys, and inclined planes. You may want to read the chapter with your child.

You may also want to expand your child's understanding of machines by completing the activity below.

Thank you for your interest and support.

Estimada familia:

Su hijo o hija ha comenzado a estudiar el Capítulo 8: *Simple Machines.* En este capítulo, su aprendemos cómo la fuerza crea movimiento con el uso de palancas, ruedas, ejes, poleas y planos inclinados. Para que su hijo o hija repase lo que ha aprendido, pueden leer juntos el capítulo y completar la actividad que presentamos a continuación.

Muchas gracias por su apoyo e interés.

Sincerely,/Atentamente,

A Tour of Machines

Talk with your child about simple machines we use as toys and sports equipment. Ask your child to explain how force makes a baseball soar. Ask your child why work is easier when we use wheels on a skateboard, ride a see-saw, or slide down a slide.

Máquinas por todas partes

Converse con su hijo o hija sobre algunas máquinas sencillas que usamos en los deportes o como juguetes. Pídale que explique cómo hace la fuerza para que una pelota de beísbol vuele. Pregúntele por qué se facilita el trabajo si andamos en una patineta con ruedas, montamos en un sube y baja o nos deslizamos por un tobogán.

© Harcourt Achieve Inc. All rights reserved. *Focus on Science Level E*